INSECTOS
INSECTS

This book provides bilingual materials to teach a fun and comprehensive unit on INSECTS. Included is a teacher's instruction section with details for each project along with ideas to use throughout the classroom. Discover INSECTS using skills in reading, math, and spelling. Both Spanish and English versions of each project are included in one book!

Cover Photos:
© 2003 Brand X Pictures

ISBN 1-59441-434-3

Dear Family Letter (pages 6–7)

Dear Family,

We are starting a unit on INSECTS. We will learn about different kinds of insects, including where they live and how to identify them.

Please join us by including insect discussions at home. Family discussions will help reinforce the concepts we are learning in class!

Sincerely,

Send this note home with students to let families know what is happening in the classroom. The letter introduces families to the upcoming unit on insects.

Insects Certificate (pages 8–9)

This is a great way to recognize and reward your students as they progress through the unit on insects.

Use the Insects Certificate as an incentive when students finish a defined list of projects or as a general award when the unit is complete. These certificates make a great classroom bulletin board display and provide students with take-home diplomas that they can be proud of.

Copy the certificates onto colorful paper or let students color their own certificates as a classroom art project.

Insect Cards (pages 10–12)

The insect cards included in this book can be used in a variety of ways to create fun and interesting learning flash cards.

bee

FLASH CARDS

Make different flash card decks of varying degrees of difficulty to use as assessment tools. Display transparencies of the cards for reference during classroom discussions.

ASSEMBLY INSTRUCTIONS

Copy the desired insect cards onto sturdy paper and cut out. Copy the English cards on one side and the Spanish cards on the other side. Laminate the cards for permanent use in the classroom or make sets for each student to use at home.

ant

CONCENTRATION

This ever-popular game helps children develop memory and matching skills. Concentration works best when played in small groups.

There are several variations of "Insect Concentration." Younger students can match picture cards to the same picture cards. Increase difficulty by mixing and matching combinations.

ASSEMBLY INSTRUCTIONS

Copy the desired insect cards onto sturdy paper and cut out. Laminate the cards for permanent use.

HOW TO PLAY

1. Mix up cards and place them facedown in rows.
2. Have students take turns choosing two cards at a time. If a student chooses two cards that match, she takes another turn. If there is no match, the next player takes a turn. The player with the most matched pairs wins the game!

Bulletin Board Strips

(pages 13–15)

Enlarge the strips to make insect bulletin board borders. Create borders for specific insect themes such as "flying insects" or "crawling insects." Have students color the pictures on the strips.

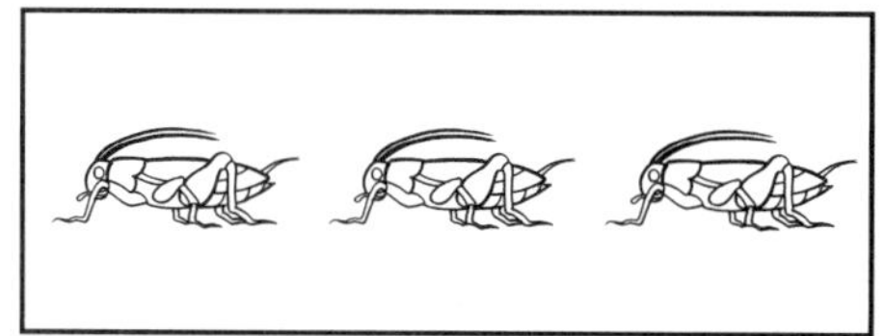

Insect Mobiles (pages 16–17)

This fun art project reinforces the skills and vocabulary learned in the insects unit. Use the mobiles as classroom decorations or to identify centers that focus on specific types of insects.

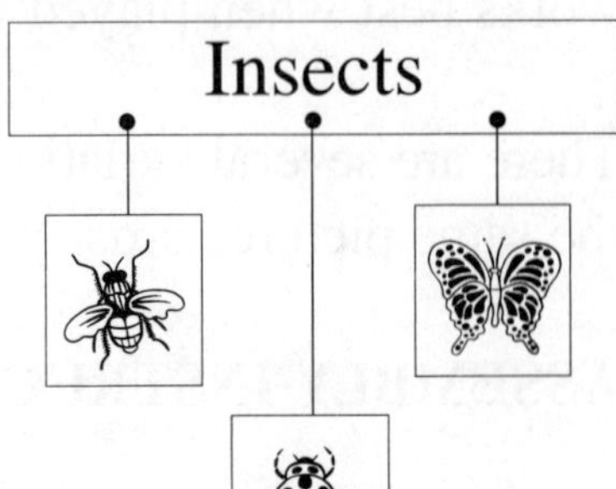

ASSEMBLY INSTRUCTIONS

Select a "header card" and the desired insect cards (pages 10–12) for a mobile and copy onto sturdy paper. Provide crayons, paint, or markers and have students color their mobile pieces. After coloring, have students fold and punch holes as indicated. Let them tape string, yarn, fishing line, or dental floss to the backs of the word cards. Then, have them glue the coordinating picture card on the back of each word card. When the glue dries, let them tie the insect cards to the header cards. Hang the mobiles from the ceiling or in a window.

Venn Diagrams (pages 18–21)

This book includes essential Venn diagram reproducibles. Use them as transparencies to aid in classroom discussions or give one copy to each student to complete. This is an excellent project to teach the differences and similarities between insects and to assess your students' listening and comprehension skills.

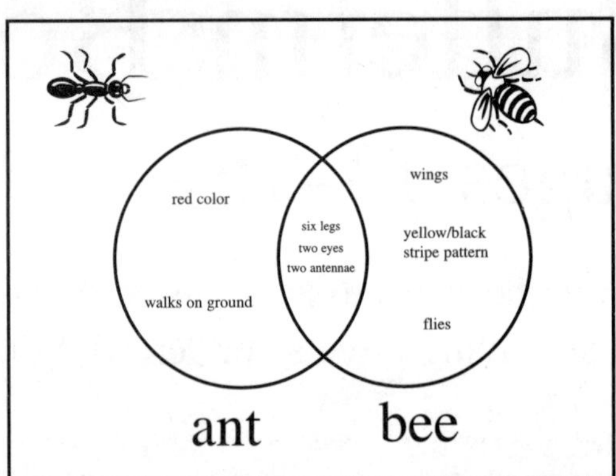

Sentence Strips (pages 22–31)

The sentence strips reinforce basic concepts presented throughout the insect unit. The strips may be used in bulletin board displays, centers, pocket charts, and as examples for story-starter books.

Insects have	two eyes.

An insect has three	body parts: the head,	thorax, and abdomen.

My Insect Books (pages 32–41)

Students can create and color their own insect books. Have students use the insect picture cards (page 10) or draw their own insects to complete the pages provided. Students can also design their own books using covers and lined pages. Teachers can design different themes by choosing various covers and pages.

ASSEMBLY INSTRUCTIONS

Copy one book for each student. Copy cover pages onto sturdy paper and inside pages onto 8½" x 11" (21.5 cm x 30 cm) white paper. Assemble and bind books using brass fasteners or staples.

Students can write stories or facts about different insects in their insect books. Have students share their completed books with the class.

My Insect Number Book

(pages 42–49)

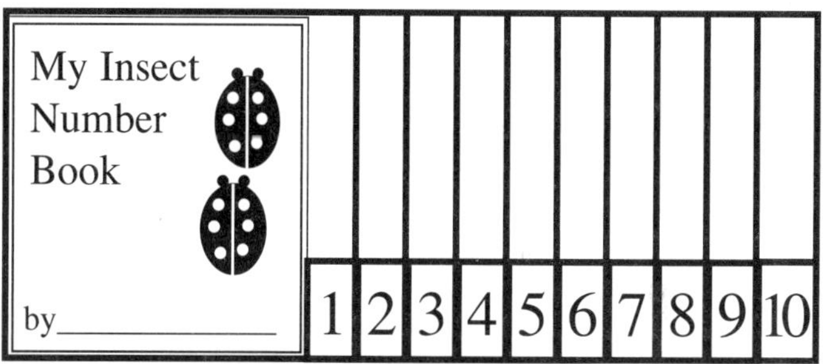

This book is a fun and interesting way to integrate insects and counting! Have students color and assemble their own books or copy each page onto colorful paper and laminate for permanent use.

Insect Anatomy Puzzles

(pages 50–53)

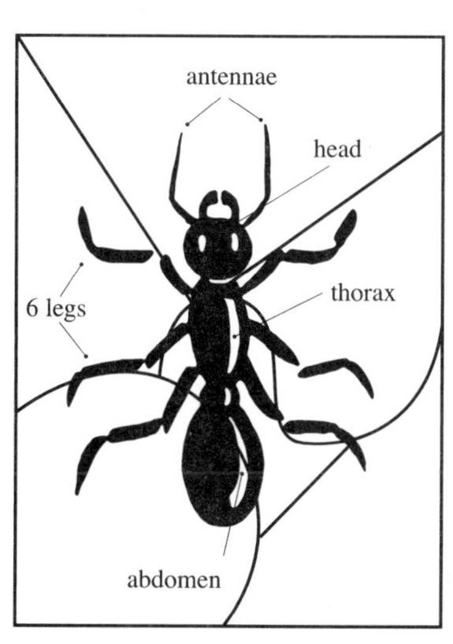

Students will love these fun, interactive insect puzzles. Copy onto tag board and cut out to create puzzles your students can use to learn about insect anatomy. This is a great center idea!

Estimada familia,

Estamos comenzando una unidad de insectos. Aprenderemos acerca de varios tipos de insectos, dónde viven y cómo se pueden identificar.

Por favor únanse a nosotros incluyendo conversaciones en casa. Las conversaciones familiares ayudan a reforzar los conceptos que se estudian en clase.

Atentamente,

Dear Family,

We are starting a unit on insects. We will learn about different kinds of insects, including where they live and how to identify them.

Please join us by including insect discussions at home. Family discussions will help reinforce the concepts we are learning in class!

Sincerely,

INSECTOS

CERTIFICADO

Nombre:______________________________

¡Felicidades!
Has aprendido
sobre los insectos.

INSECTS

CERTIFICATE

Name:________________________________

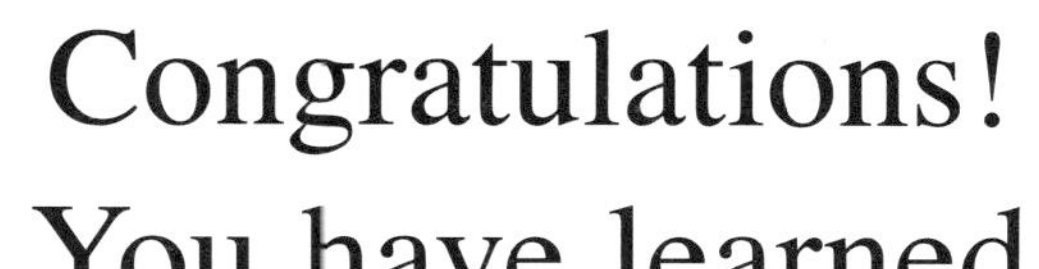

Congratulations!
You have learned
about insects.

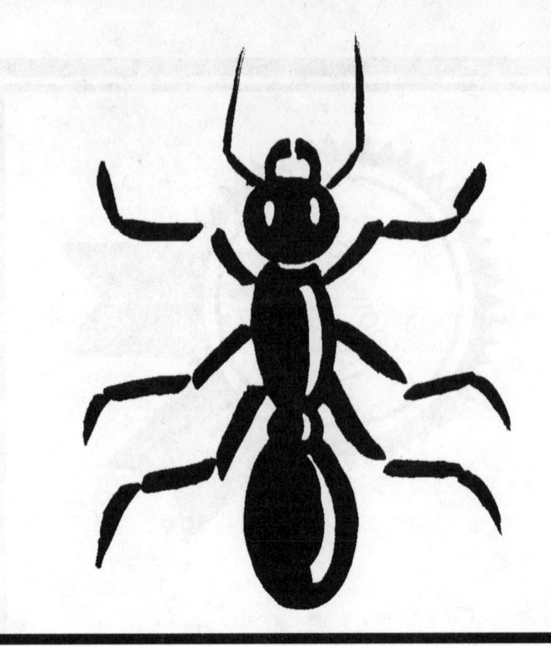

abeja

hormiga

mosca

mariposa

catarina

saltamontes

ant

bee

butterfly

fly

grasshopper

ladybug

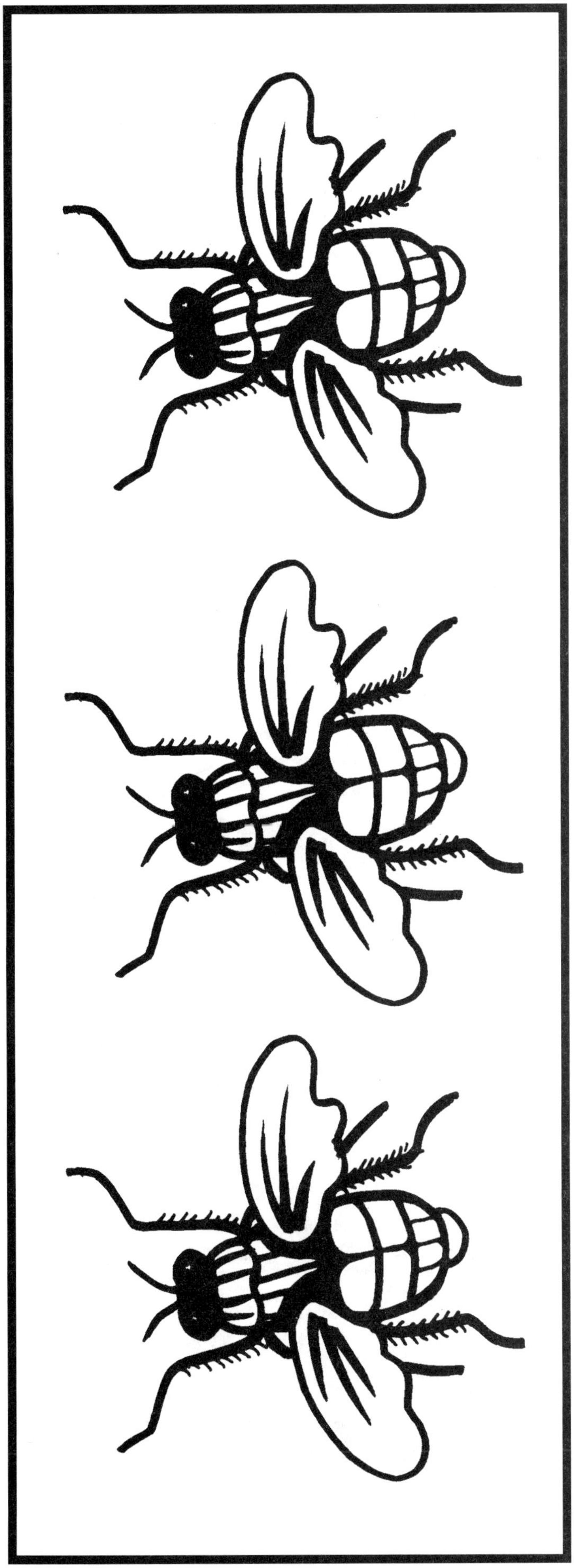

Móviles de los insectos

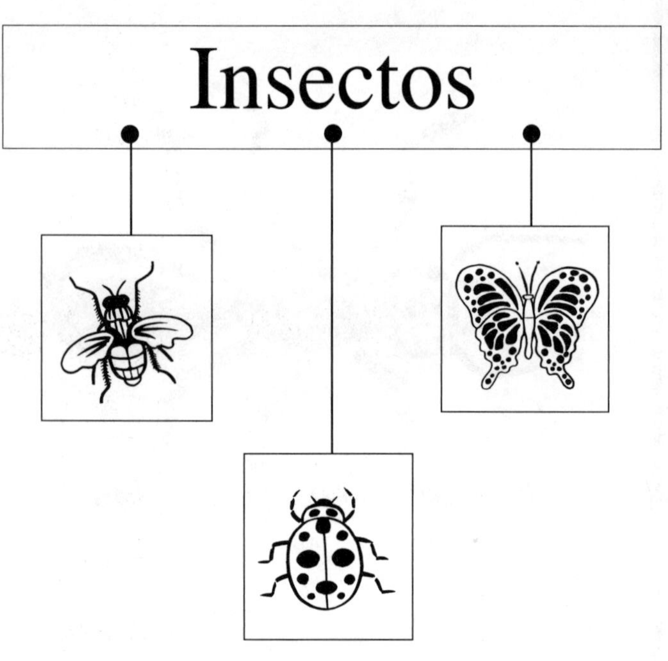

Insectos

Insectos

Insect Mobiles

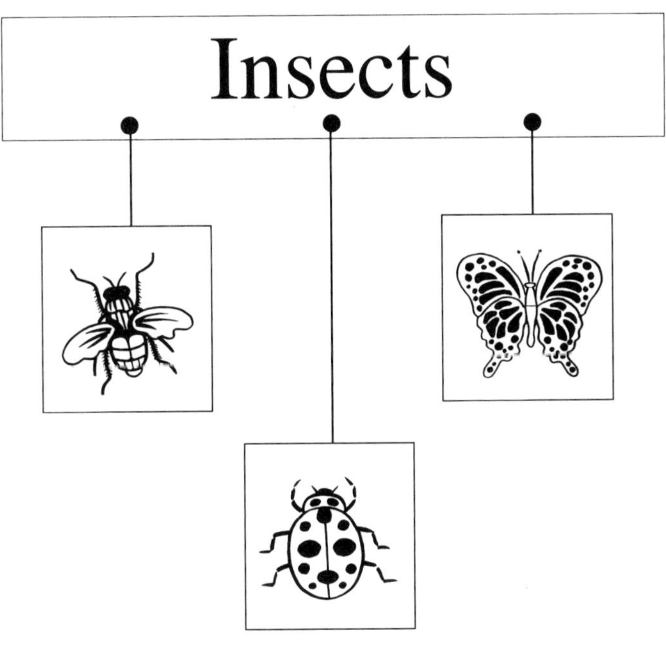

Insects

Insects

Insectos

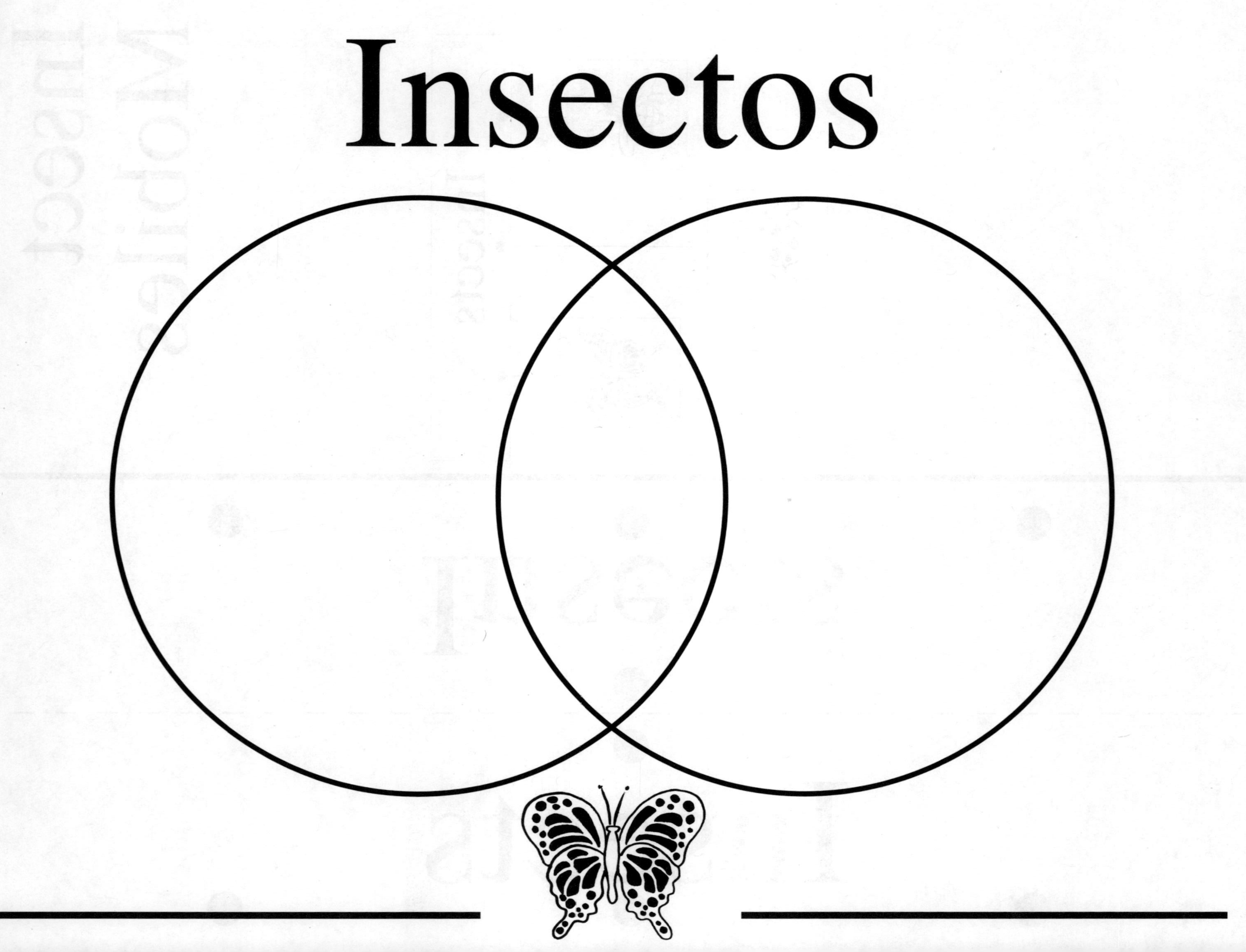

Insects

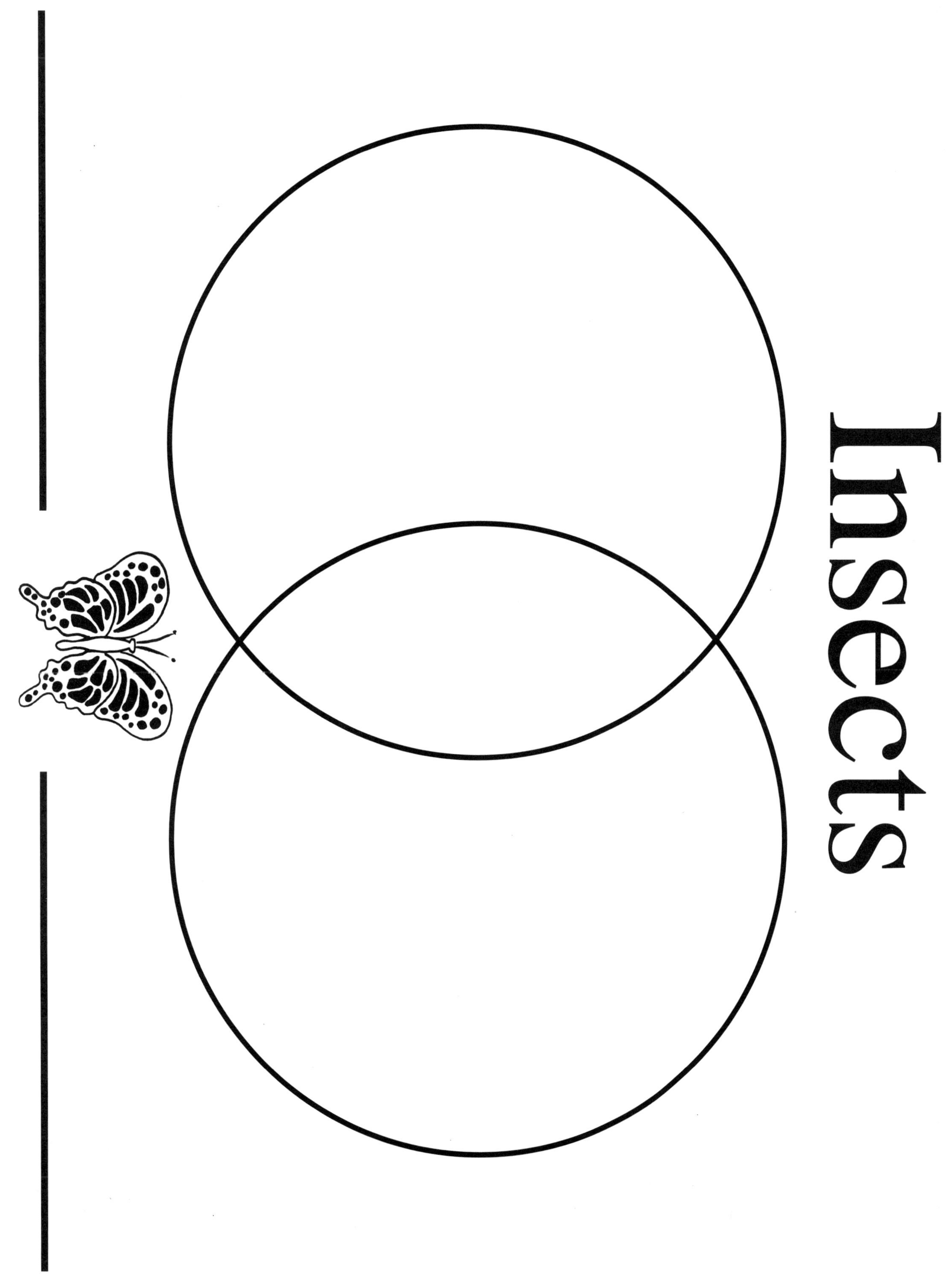

hormiga abeja

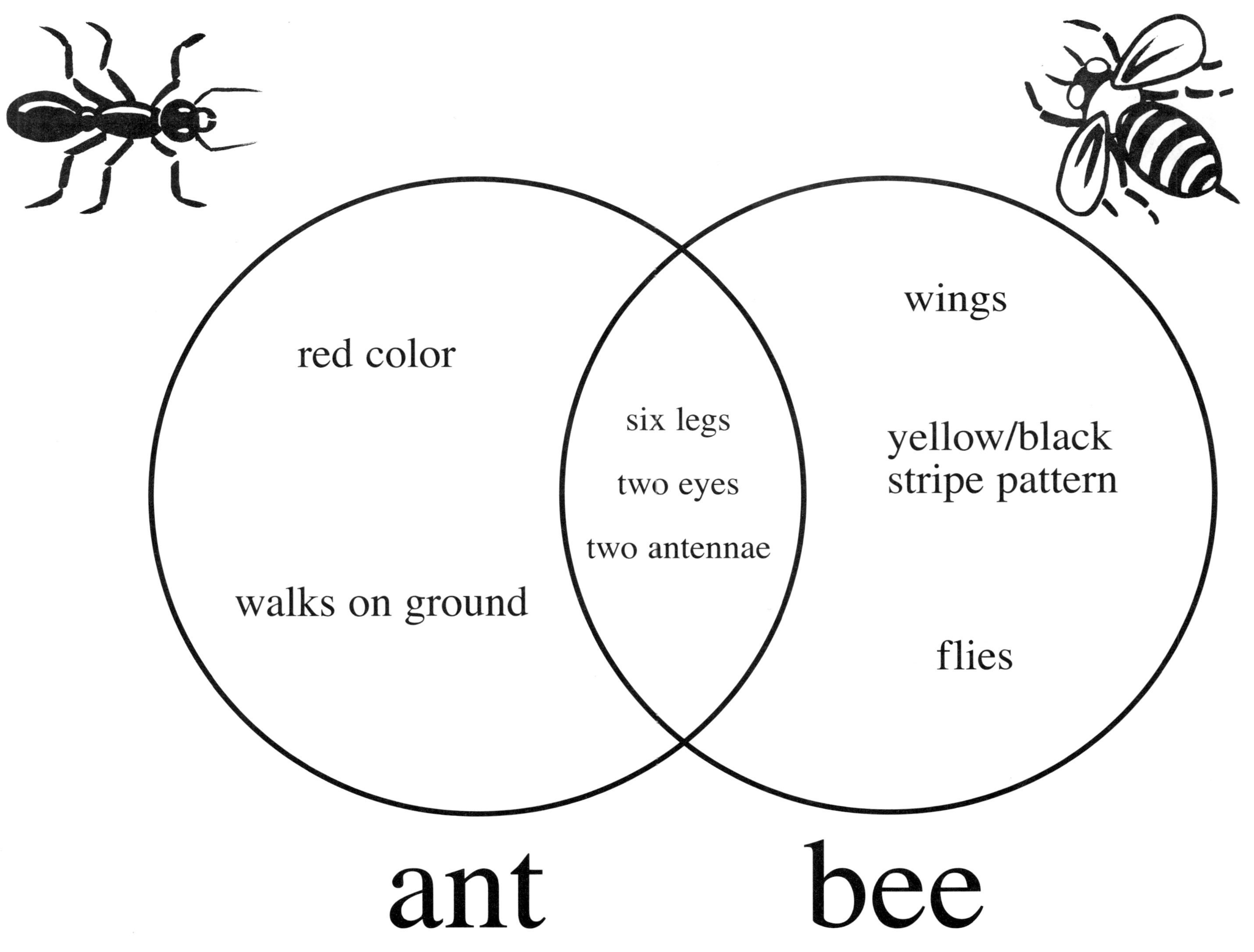
red color
walks on ground
six legs
two eyes
two antennae
wings
yellow/black
stripe pattern
flies
ant
bee

Oración en tiras

Los insectos tienen

dos ojos.

Los insectos tienen

Sentence Strips

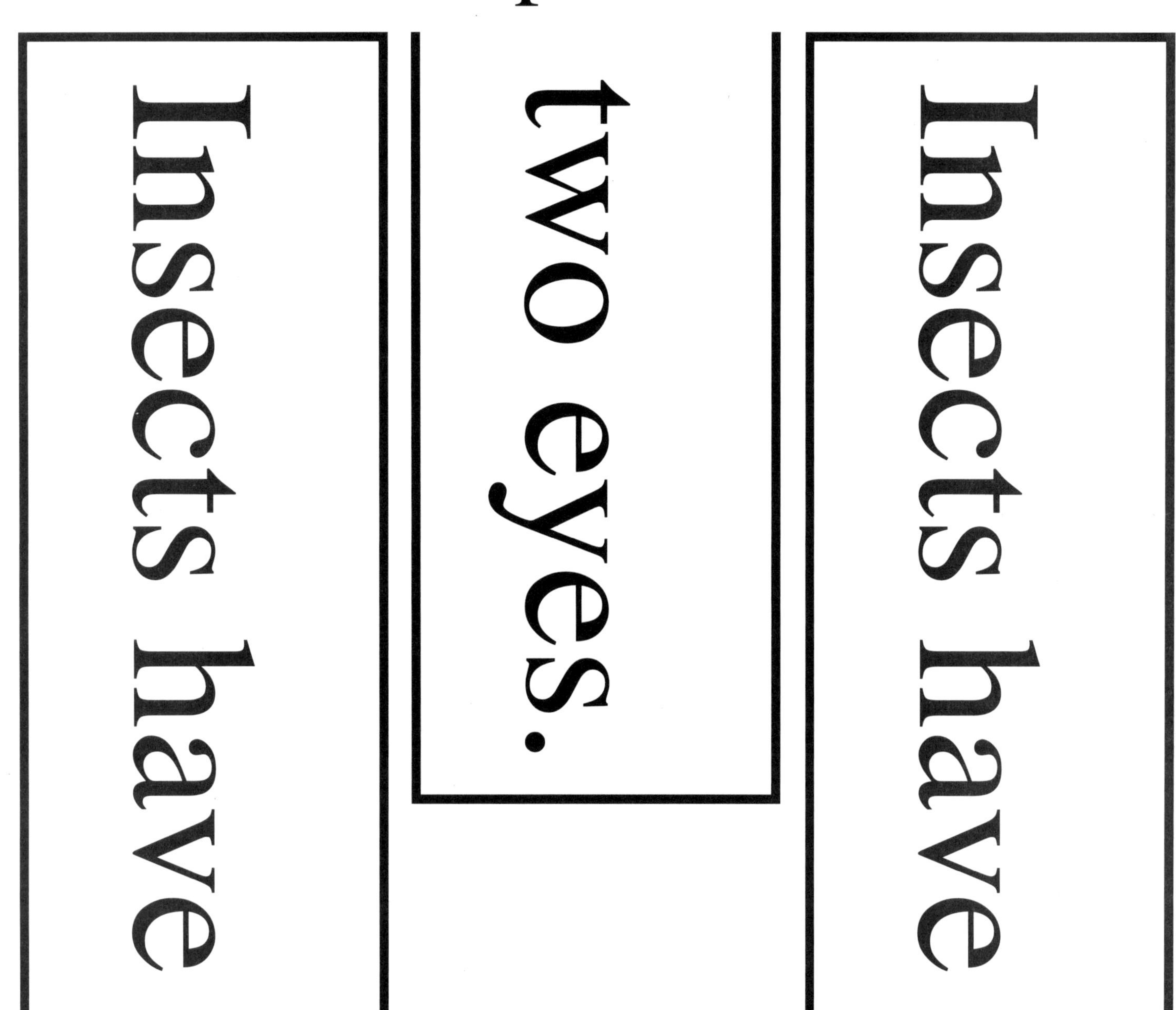

dos antenas.

Los insectos tienen

seis patas.

two antennae.

Insects have

six legs.

El cuerpo de un insecto

tiene tres partes: la cabeza,

el tórax y el abdomen.

An insect has three

body parts: the head,

thorax, and abdomen.

Hay algunos

insectos con alas.

Some insects

have wings.

Hay algunos

insectos que no

tienen alas.

There are some

insects that do

not have wings.

Este libro
fue hecho por:

Nombre: ____________________

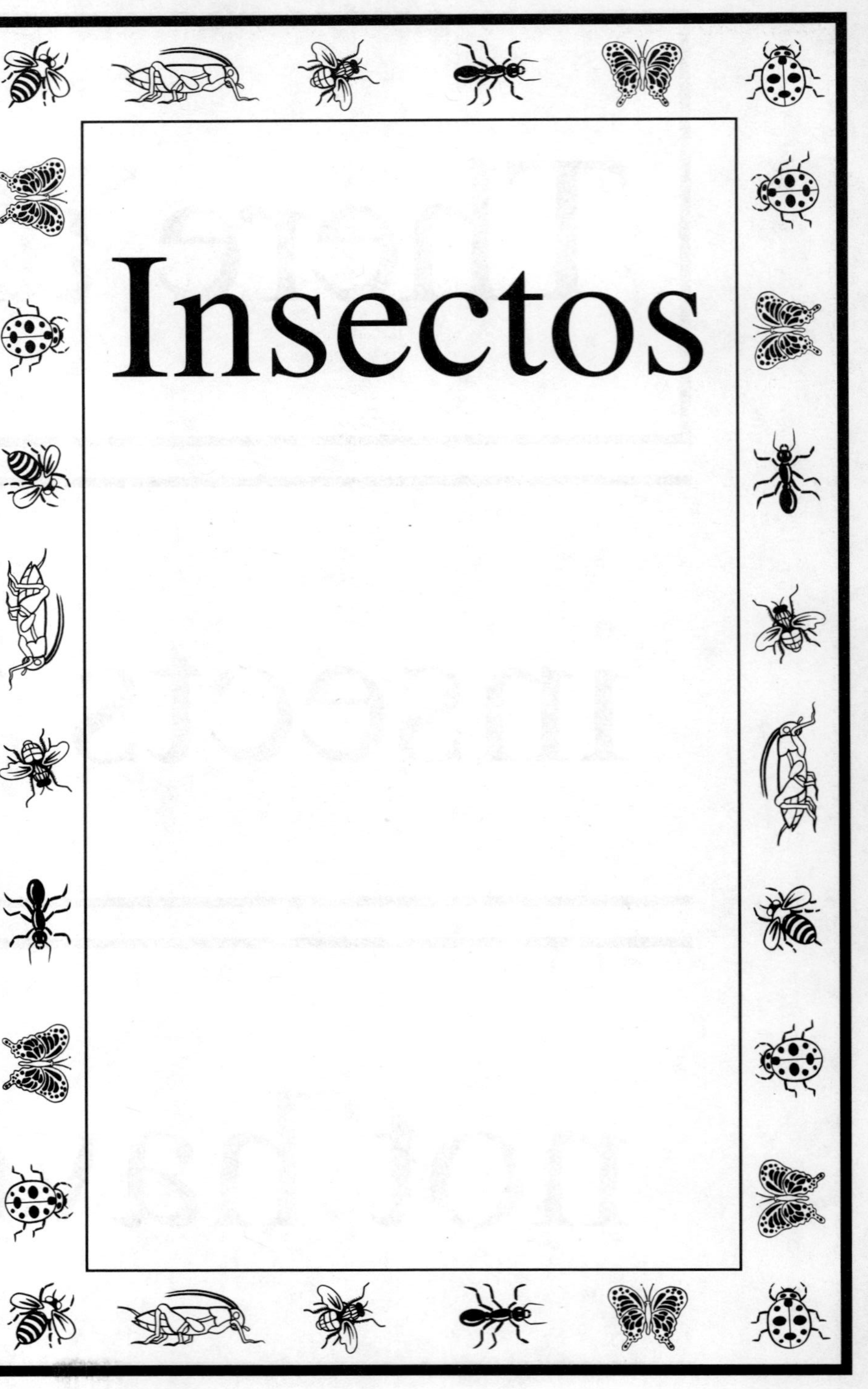

This Book Was

Created By:

Name: ______________________

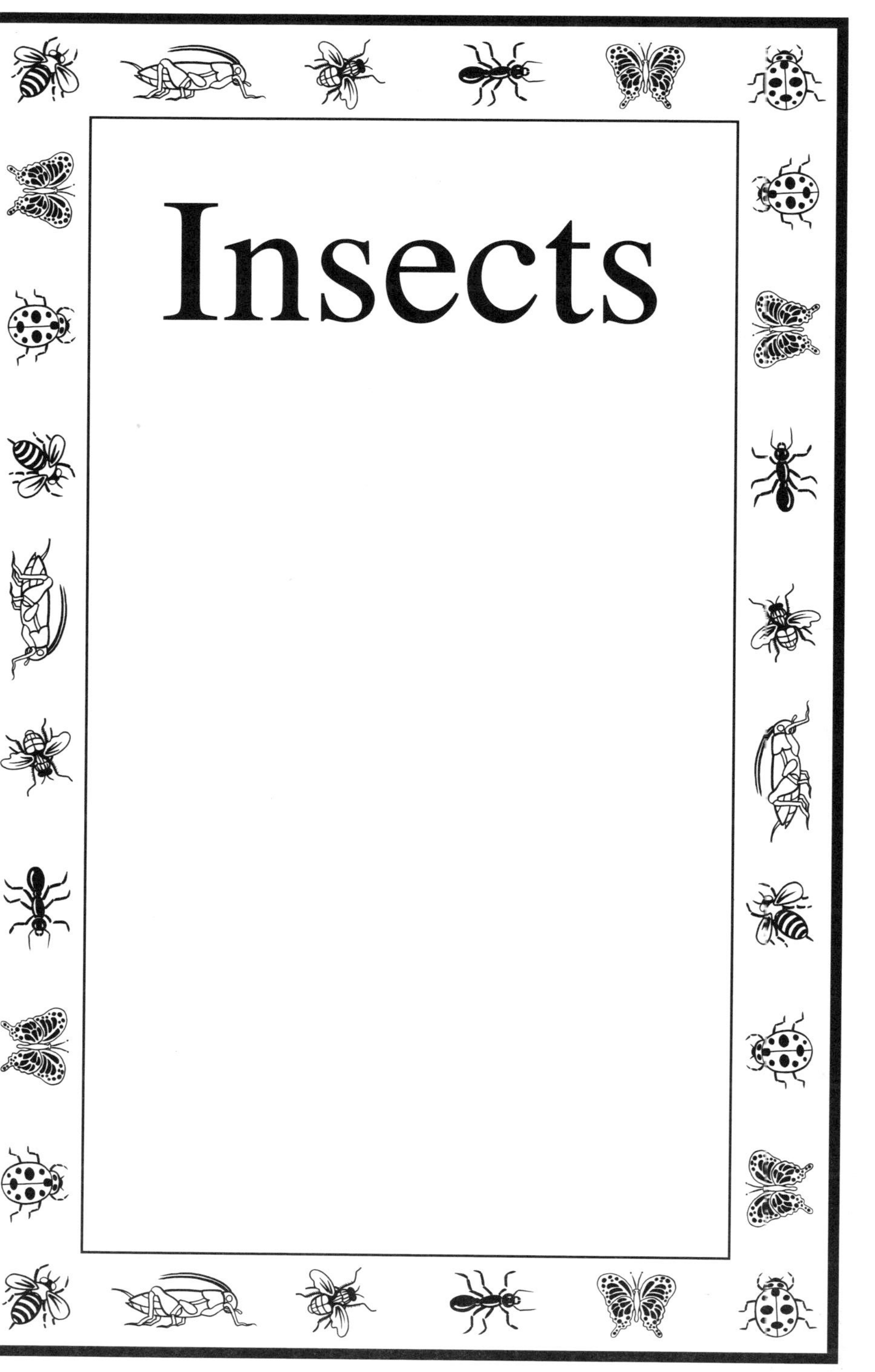

¡__________ están en todas partes!

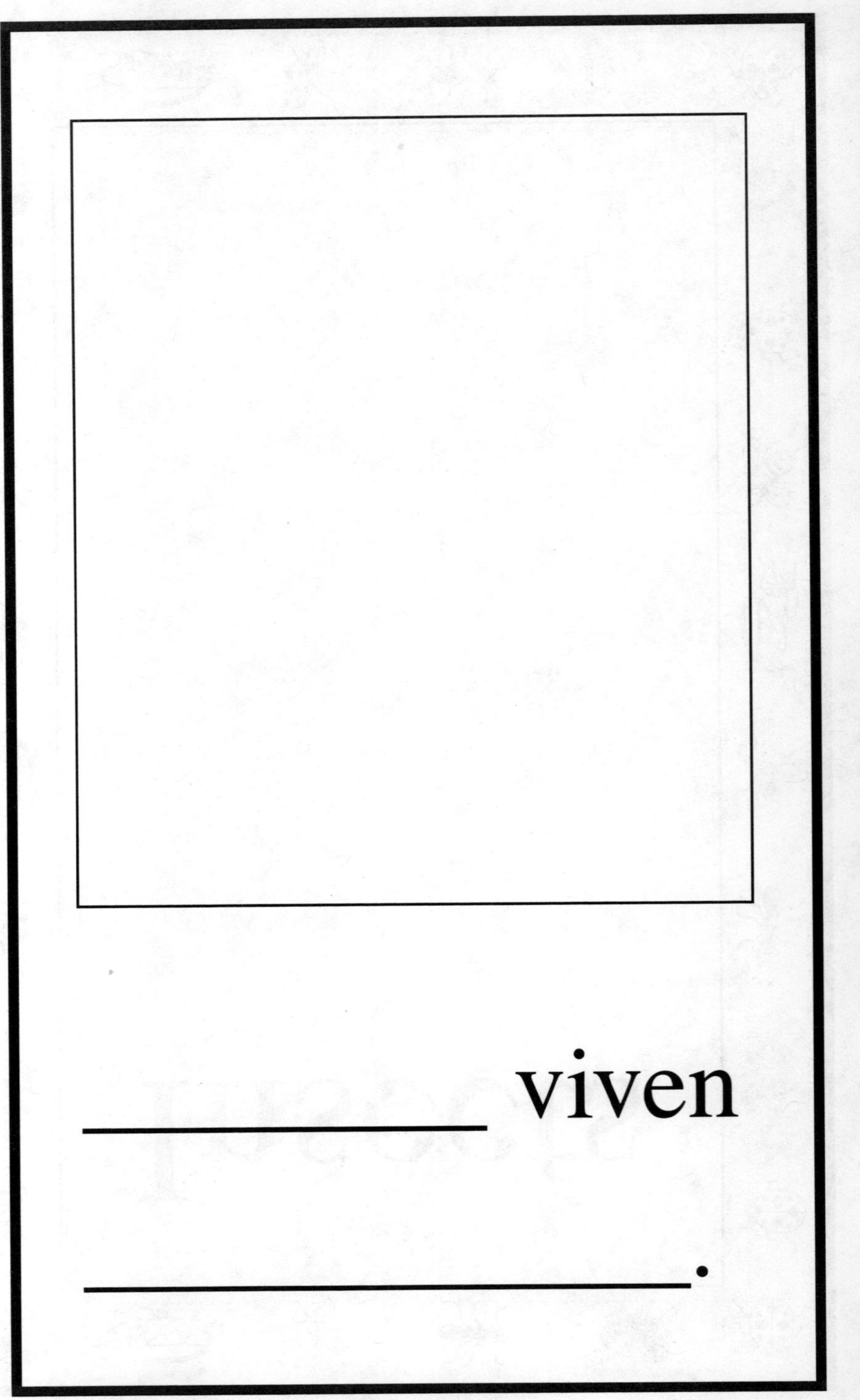

__________ viven __________.

________ are everywhere!

_____ huelen
con sus antenas.

tienen _____
patas. _____

__________ smell

with their antennae.

__________ have

__________ legs.

Los cuerpos de

______ ____________

tienen _______ partes.

____

son insectos.

__________ have

_____ body parts.

____

are insects.

Mi libro de
los numeros
sobre los
insectos

por ______________

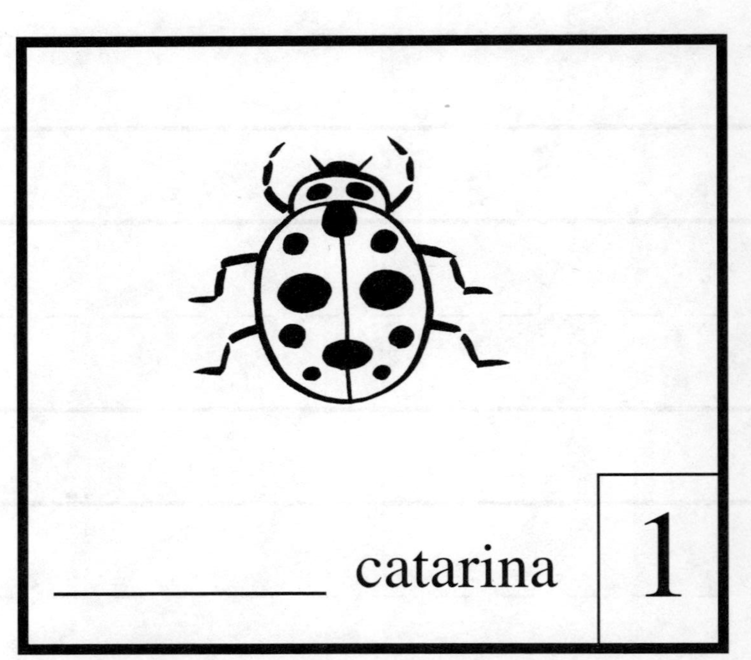

__________ catarina 1

______________ abejas 2

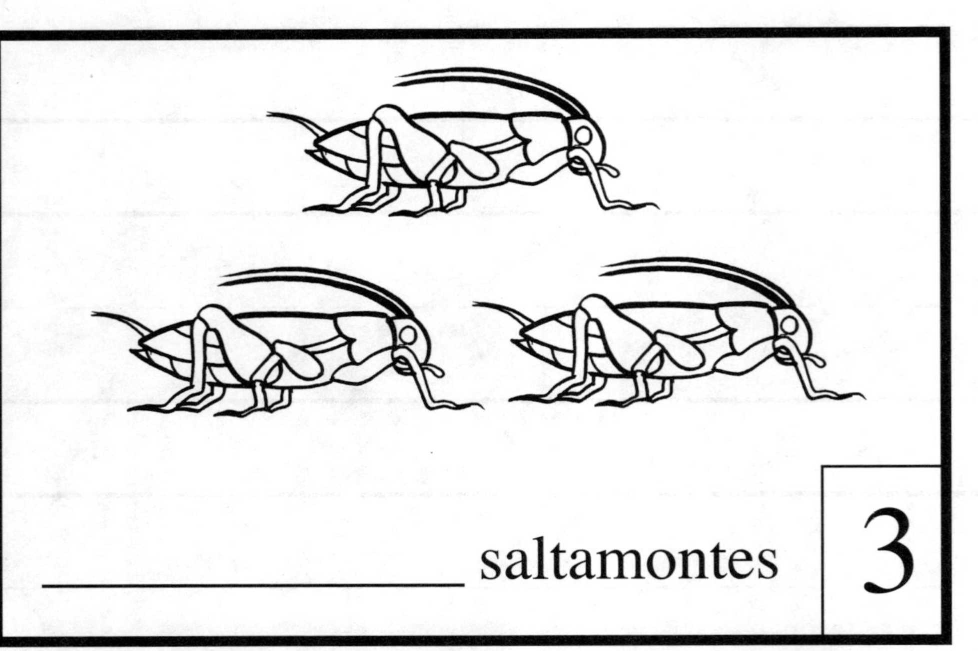

______________ saltamontes 3

bees
2

My
Insect
Number
Book
by

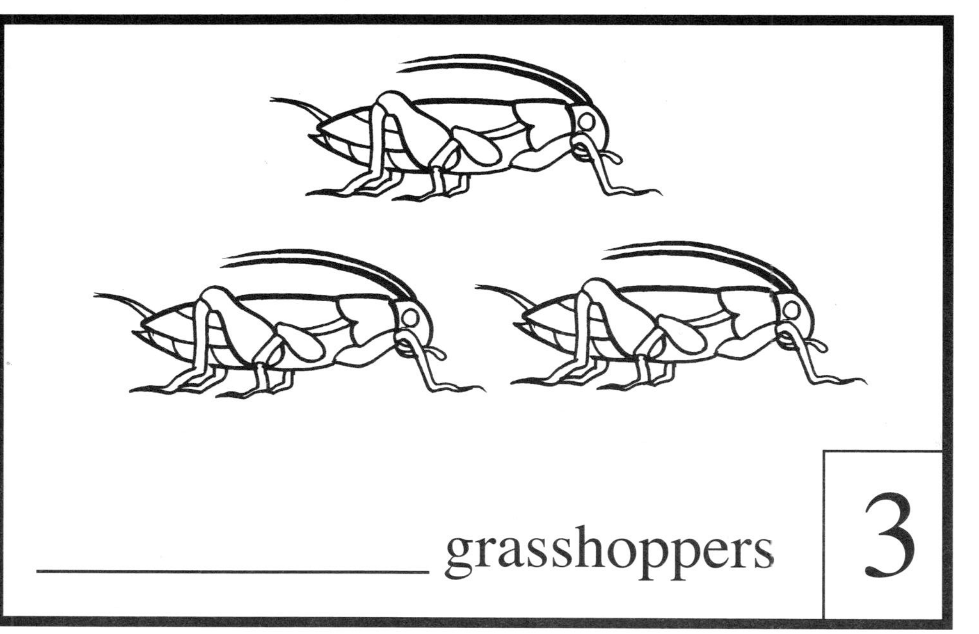
grasshoppers
3

ladybug
1

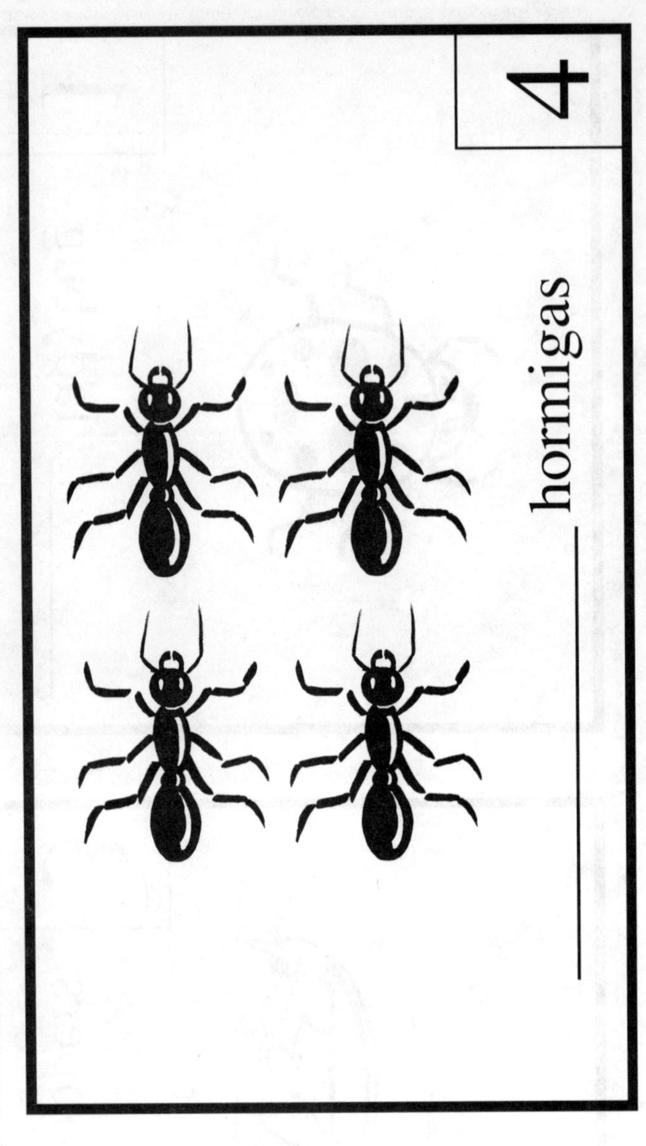
4
hormigas

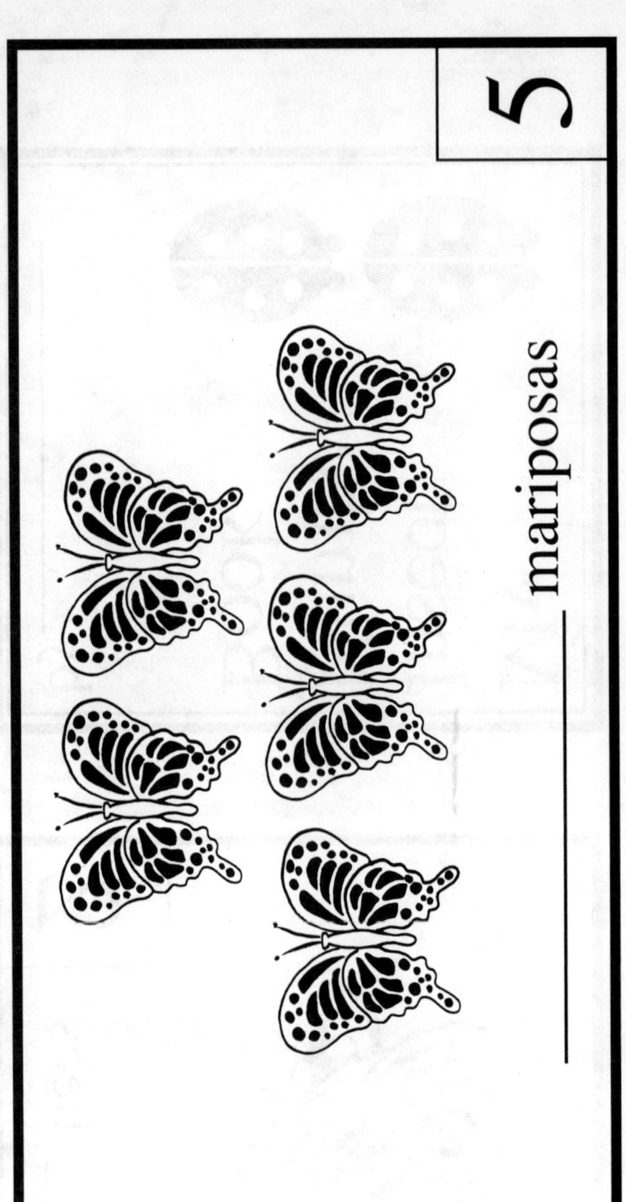
5
mariposas

moscas
6

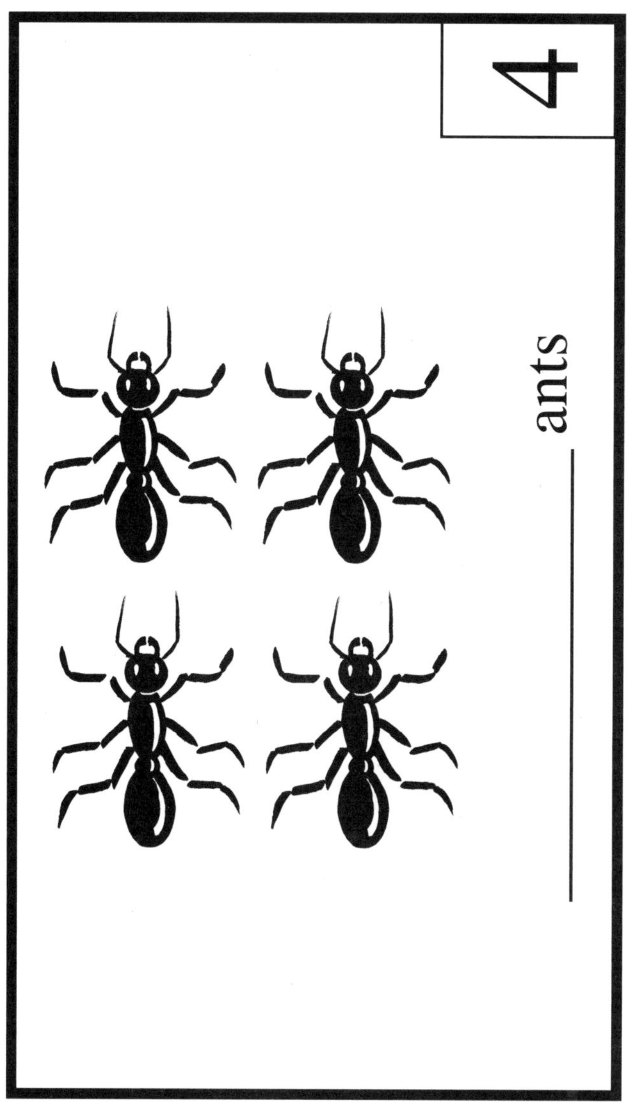
4
______ ants

5
______ butterflies

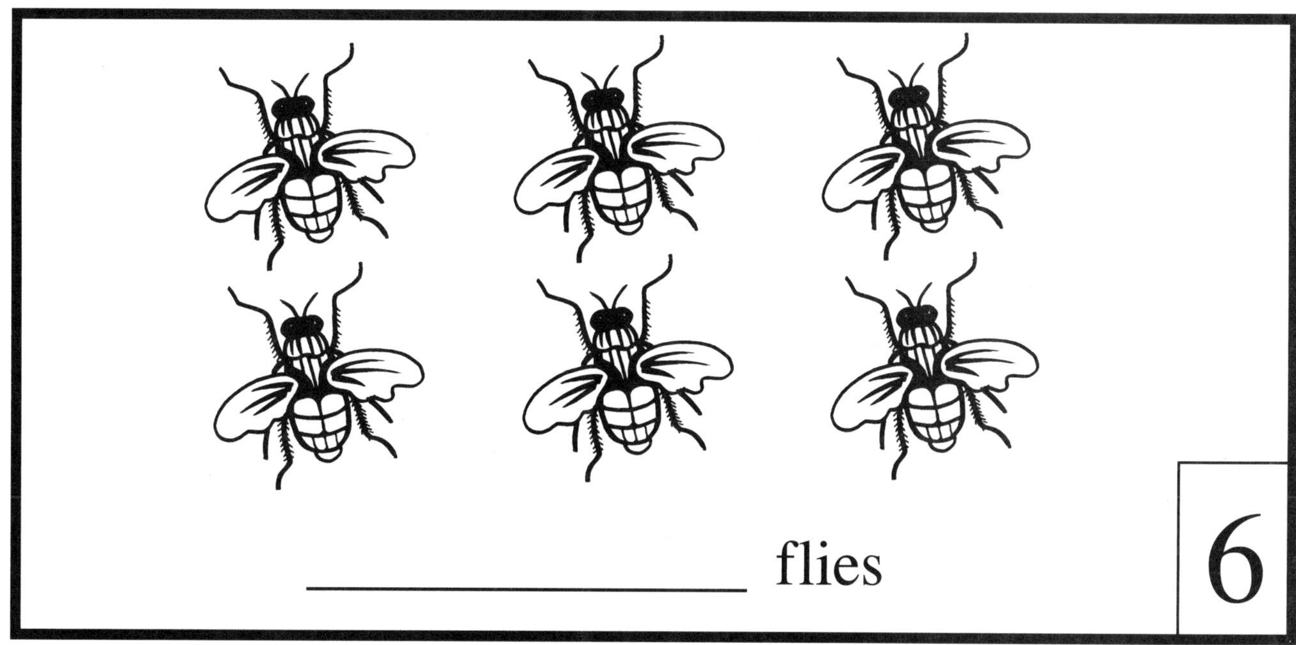
______ flies
6

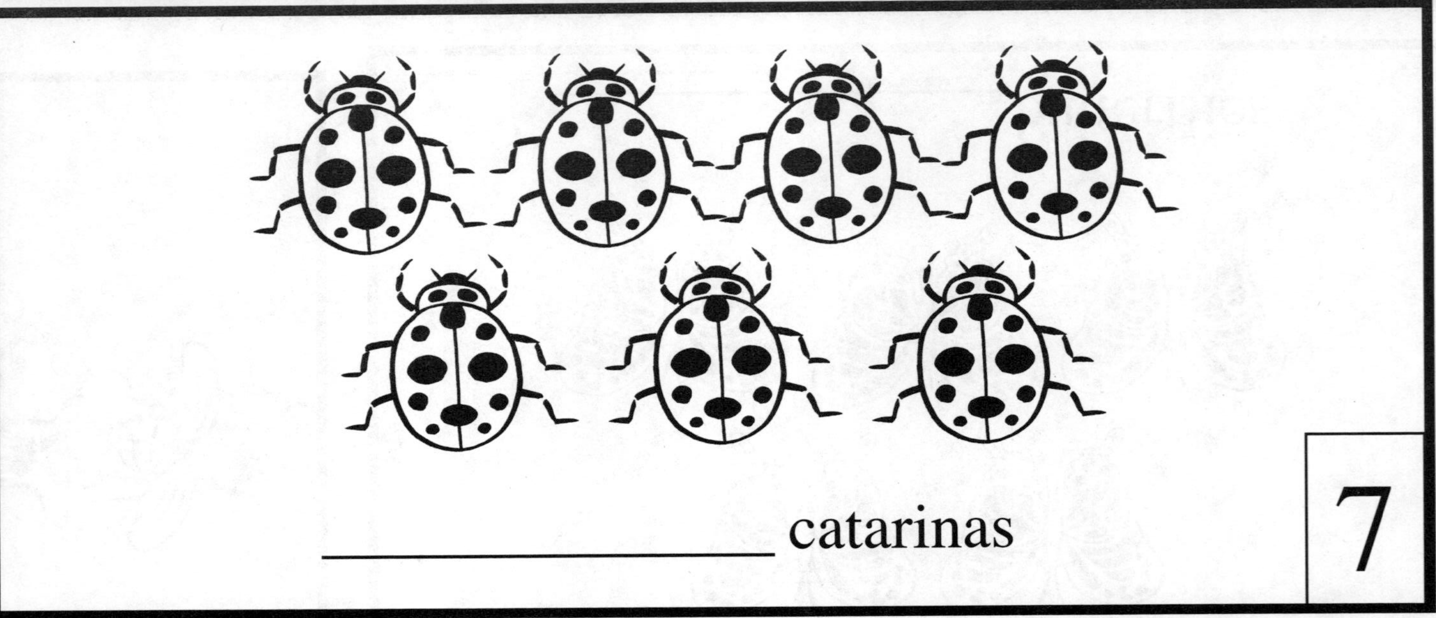
________ catarinas
7

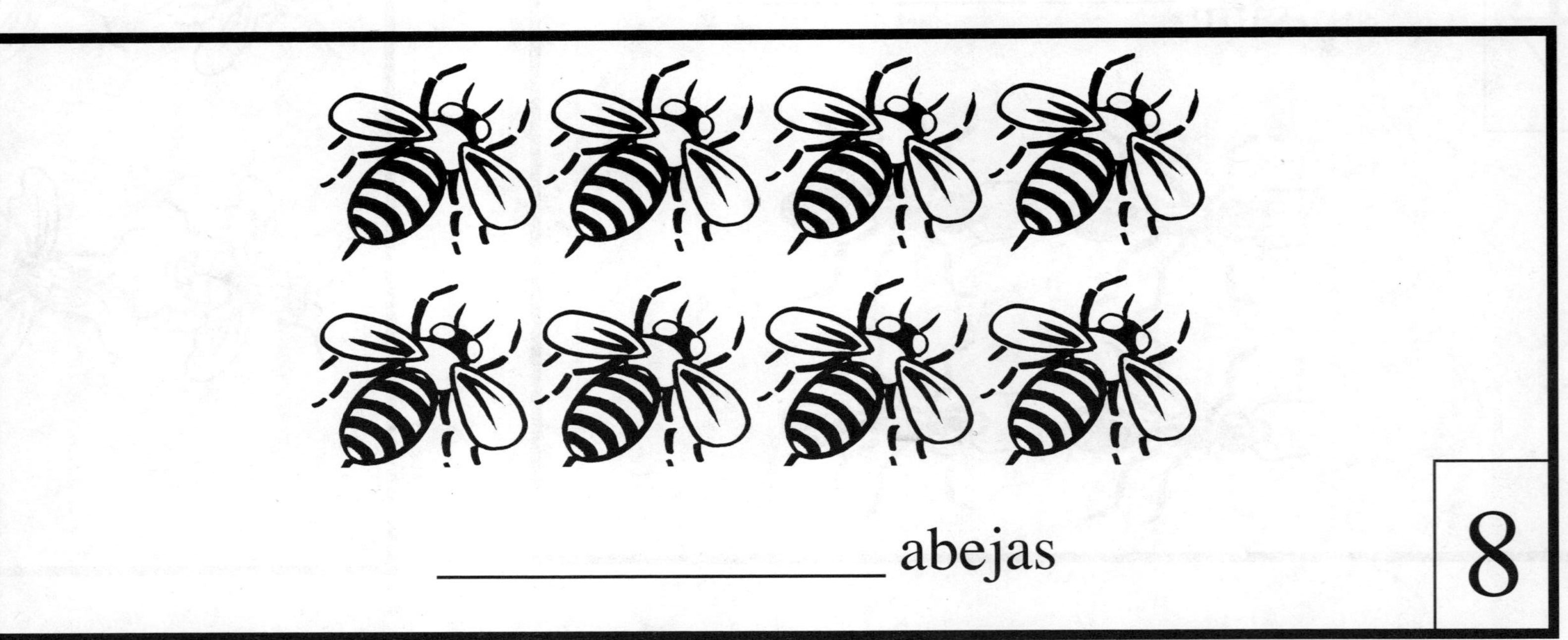
________ abejas
8

ladybugs
7

bees
8

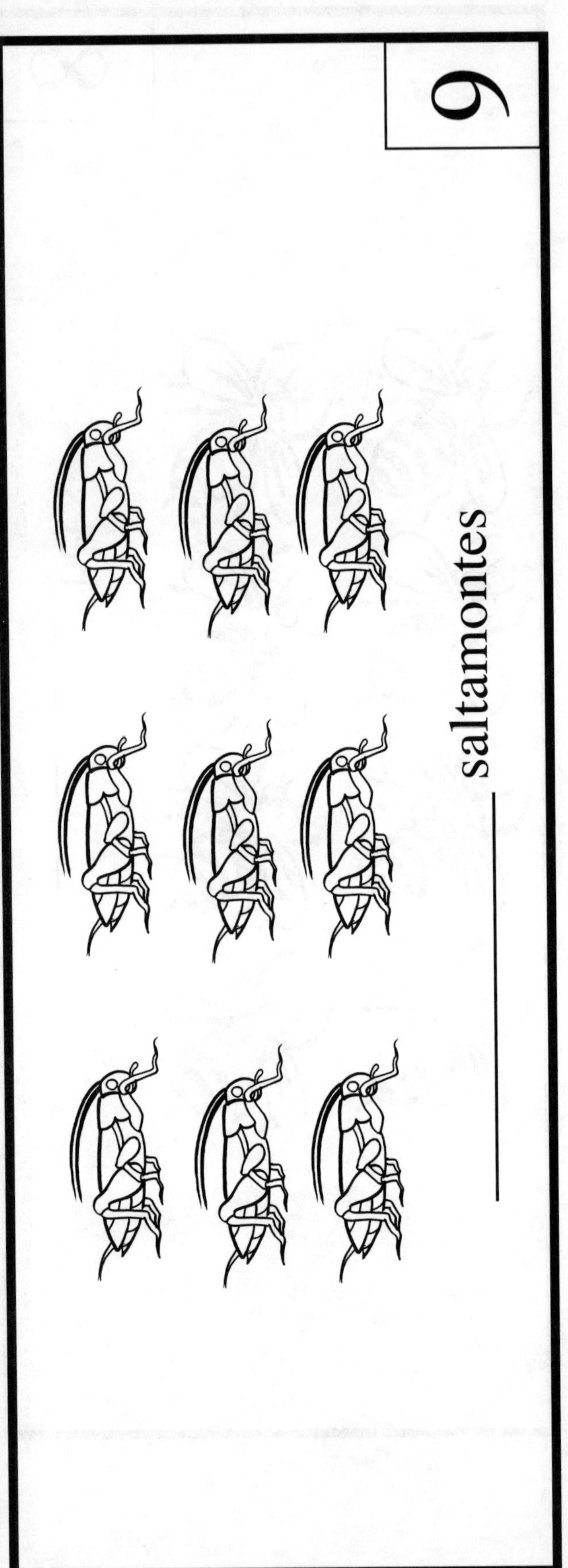

9

saltamontes ____________

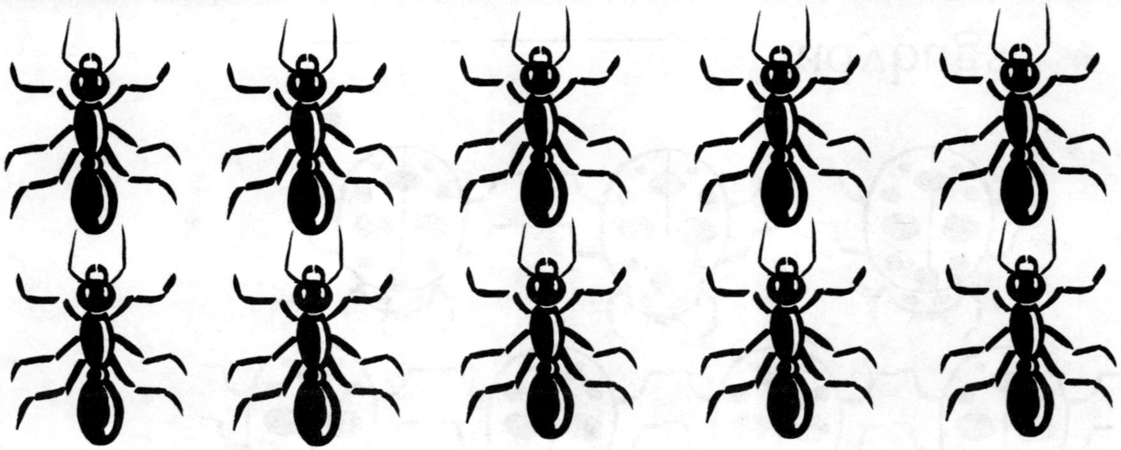

10

hormigas ____________

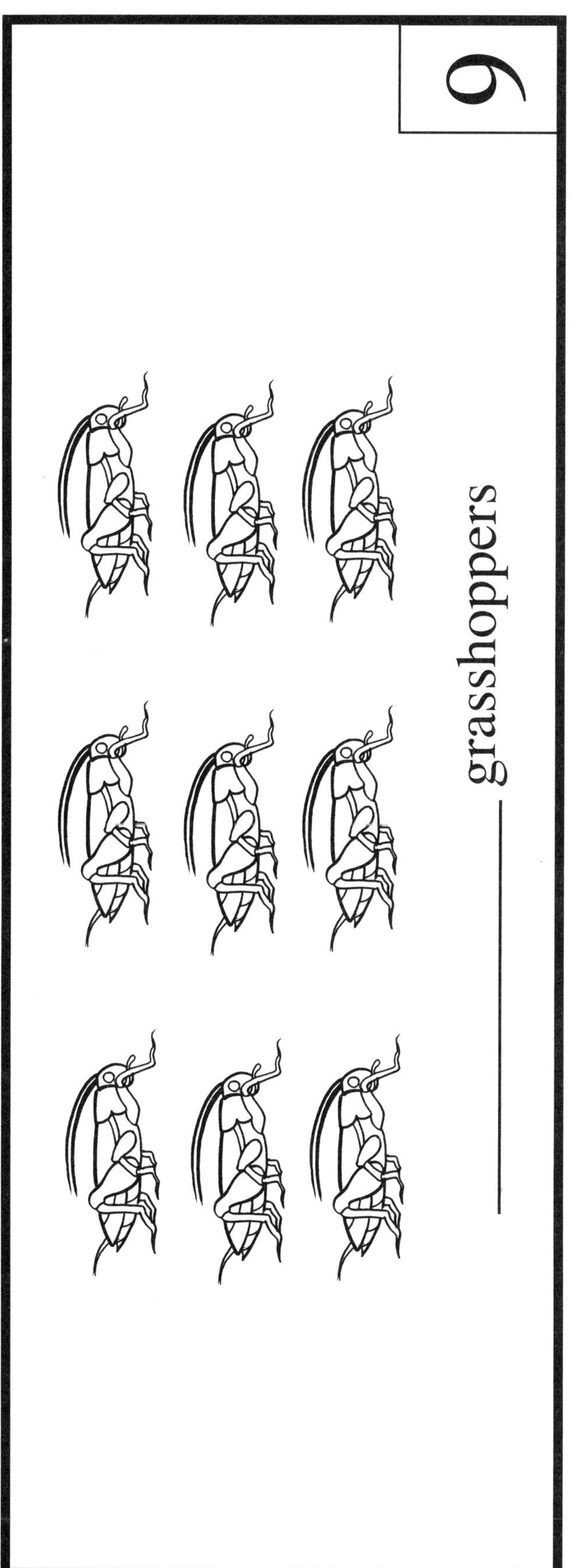

10

_______ ants

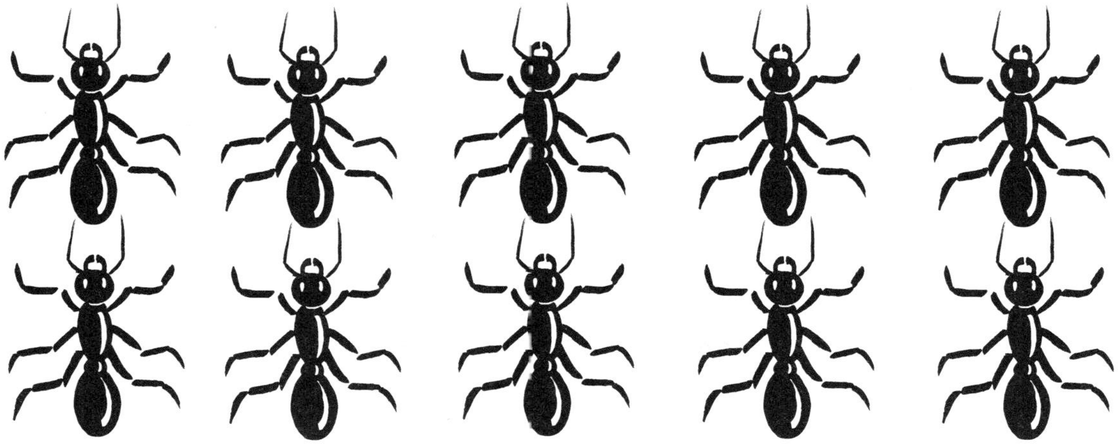

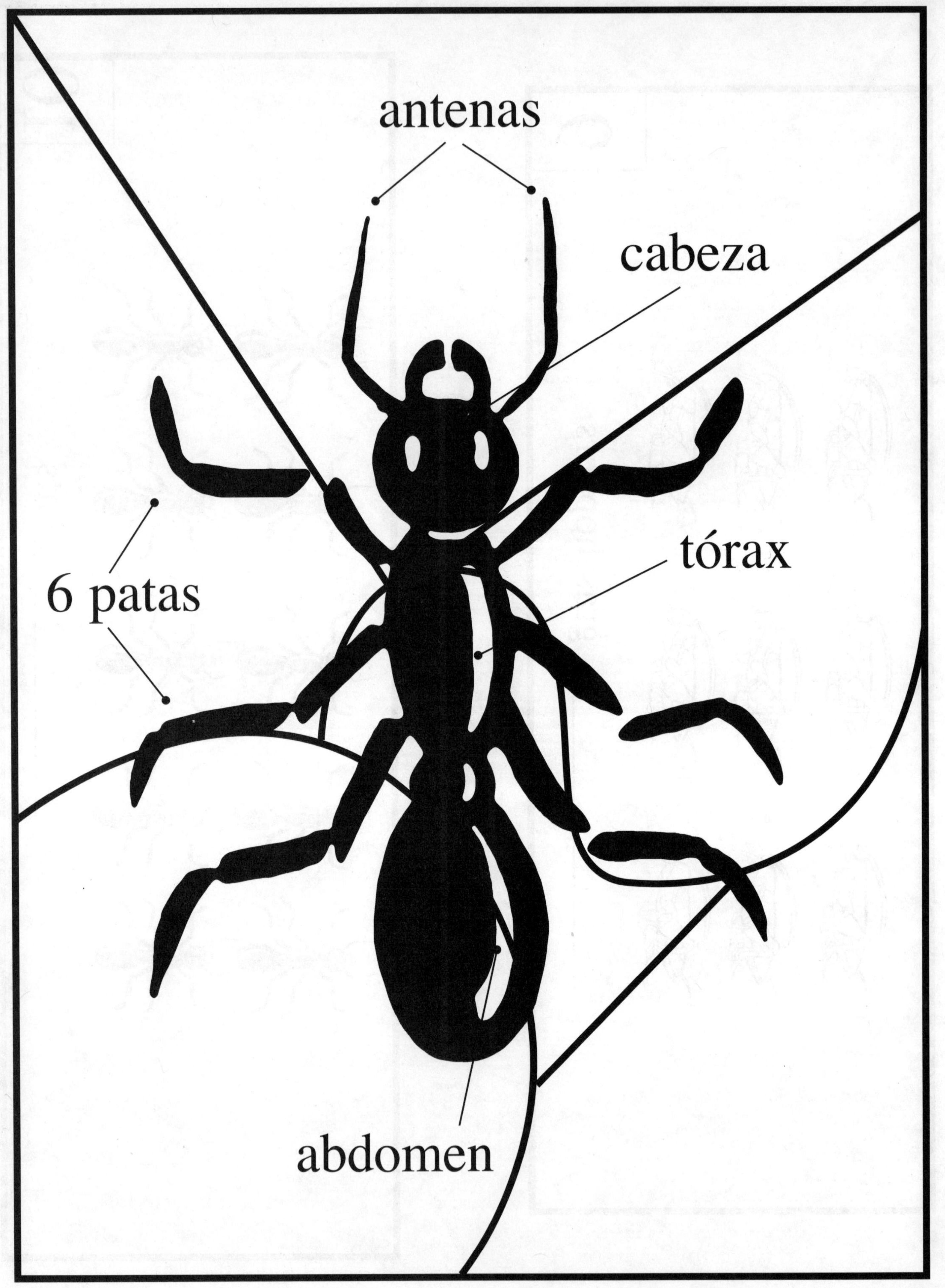
antenas
cabeza
tórax
6 patas
abdomen

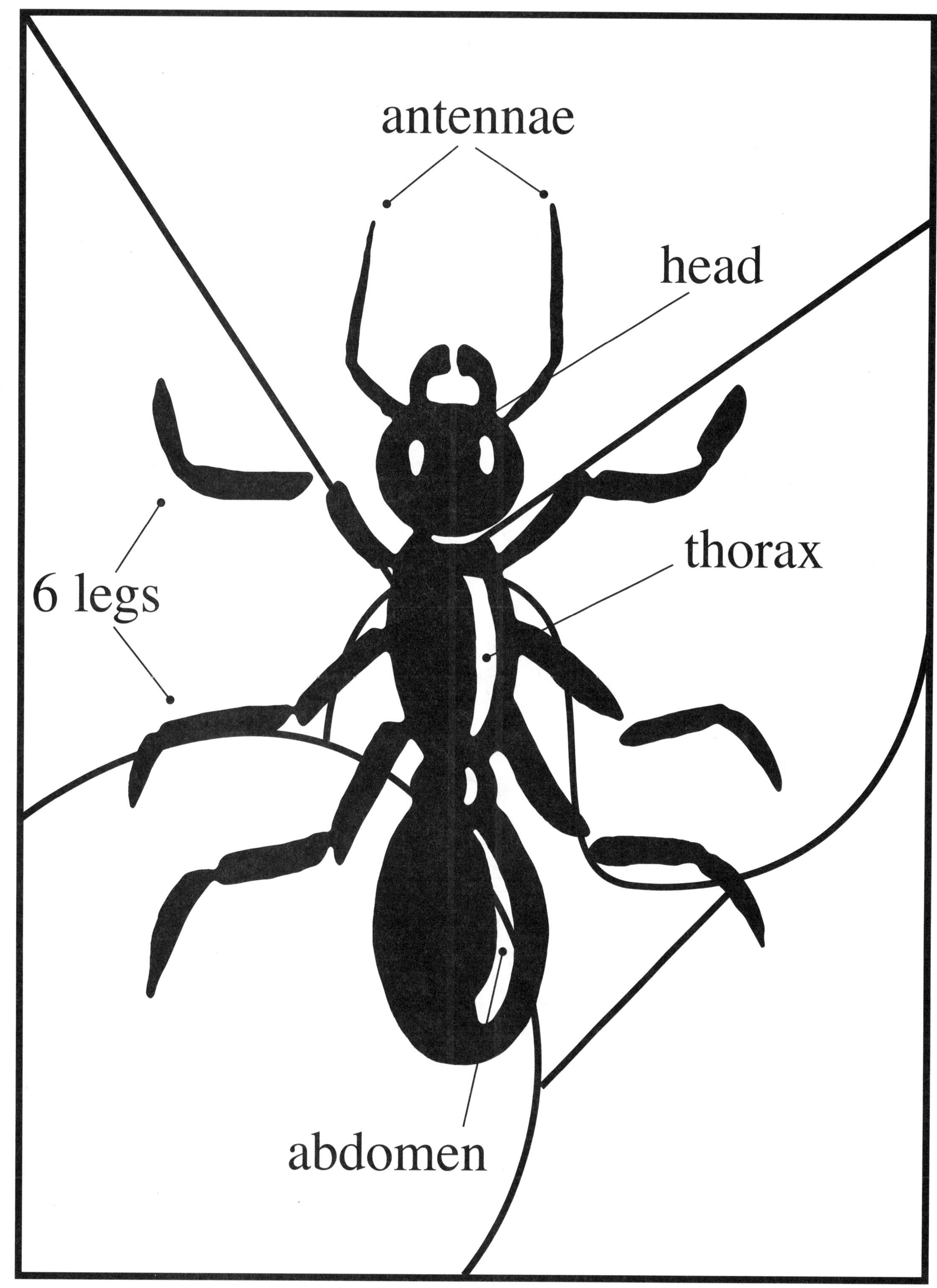
antennae
head
thorax
6 legs
abdomen

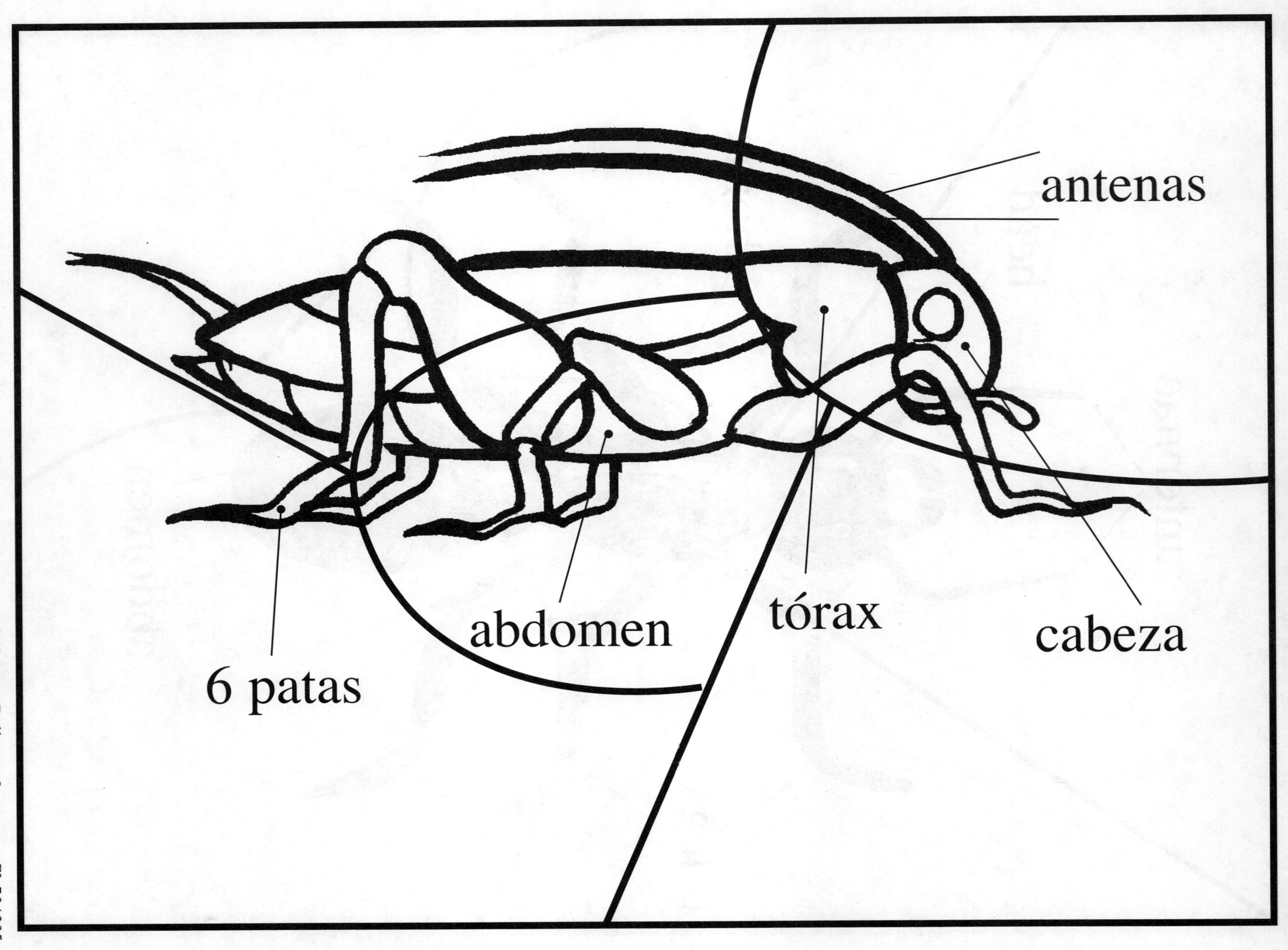
antenas
cabeza
tórax
abdomen
6 patas

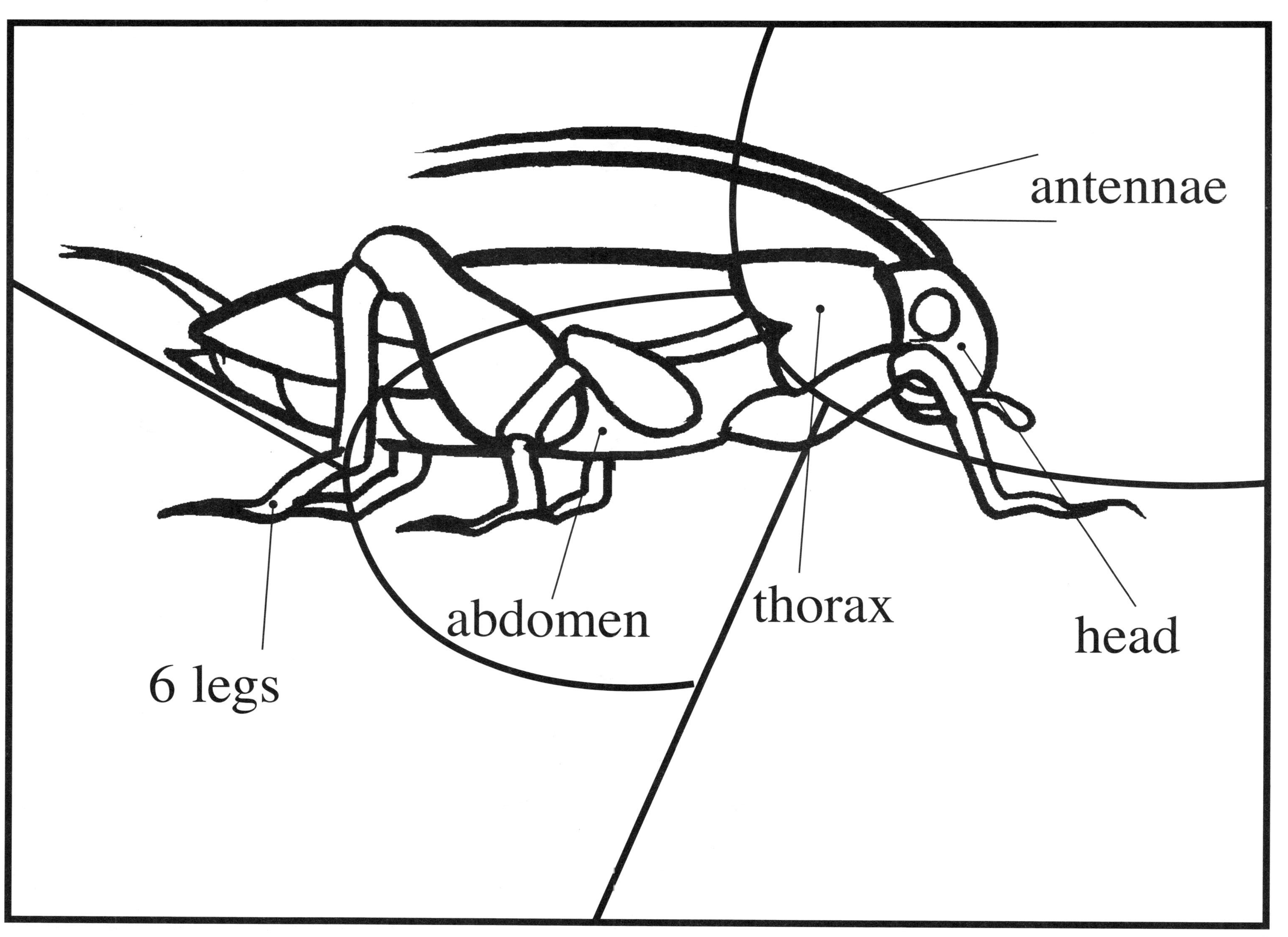
antennae
head
thorax
abdomen
6 legs

Nombre: ______________________________

Problemas de matemáticas

Resuelve cada problema y muestra tu trabajo.

1. María atrapó 10 insectos en su jardín. Se llevó 3 a la escuela. ¿Cuántos le quedaron en casa?

   ____

2. Colorea de rojo el primer insecto a tu izquierda. Colorea de azul el cuarto insecto de izquierda a derecha.

3. Eduardo tiene 7 insectos en un jarrón. Su hermano Felipe cogió 2 insectos más y los añadió al jarrón de Eduardo. ¿Cuántos insectos tiene Eduardo ahora? ¿Puedes escribir la ecuación del problema?

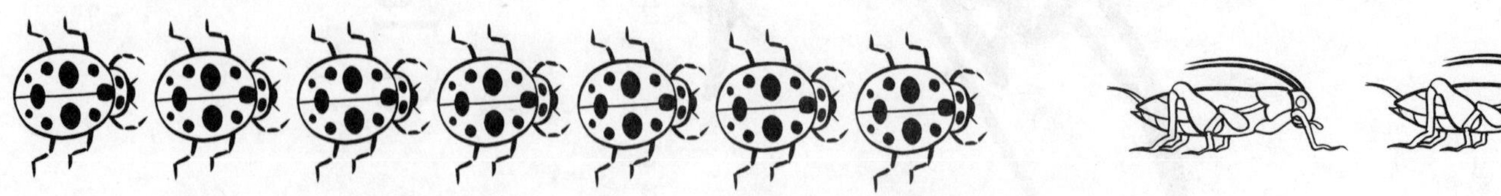

Respuesta: ____________ Ecuación: __________________

Name: ______________________________

Insect Story Problems

Answer each problem and show your work.

1. Maria caught 10 insects in her backyard. She took 3 to school. How many did Maria have left at home?

   ____

2. Starting at the left, color the first insect red. Starting at the left, color the fourth insect blue.

3. Edward has 7 insects in a jar. His brother Phil caught 2 more insects and added them to Edward's jar. How many insects does Edward have now? Can you write the equation to the above problem?

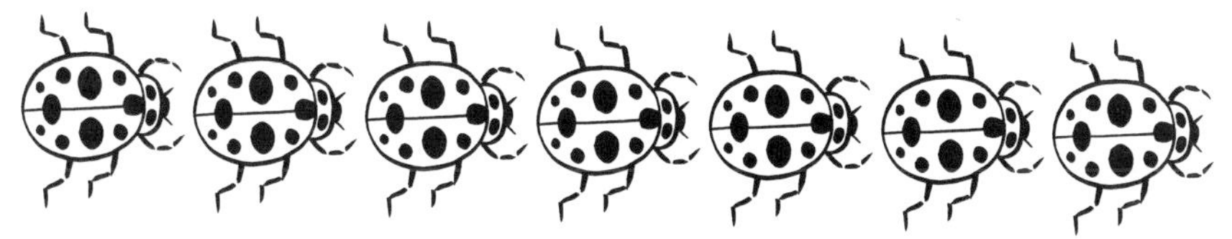

Answer: ____________ Equation: ________________

Nombre: ______________________________

El saltamontes

Responde a cada pregunta.

1. Éste es un saltamontes. ¿Cuántas patas tiene un saltamontes? (Haz un círculo.)

   seis tres ocho

2. ¿Cuántas alas tiene un saltamontes? (Haz un círculo.)

   cuatro tres ocho

3. Haz un círculo alrededor de la cabeza del saltamontes.

4. Colorea el abdomen del saltamontes de verde y el tórax de rojo.

5. ¿Vuela el saltamontes? ________________

Name: ______________________________

Grasshopper

Answer each question.

1. This is a grasshopper. How many legs does a grasshopper have? (Circle one.)

   six three eight

2. How many wings does a grasshopper have? (Circle one.)

   four three eight

3. Circle the head of the grasshopper.

4. Color the abdomen of the grasshopper green and the thorax red.

5. Does the grasshopper fly? ________________

Nombre: ______________________________

La catarina

Responde a cada pregunta.

1. Ésta es una catarina. ¿Cuántas patas tiene una catarina? (Haz un círculo.)

   seis   dos   cero

2. ¿Cuántos ojos tiene una catarina? (Haz un círculo.)

   seis   dos   cero

3. Haz un círculo alrededor de la cabeza de la catarina.

4. Colorea el abdomen de la catarina de verde y el tórax de azul.

5. ¿Vuela la catarina? ________________

Name: ______________________________

Ladybug

Answer each question.

1. This is a ladybug. How many legs does a ladybug have? (Circle one.)

   six two zero

2. How many eyes does a ladybug have? (Circle one.)

   six two zero

3. Circle the head of the ladybug.

4. Color the abdomen of the ladybug green and the thorax blue.

5. Does the ladybug fly? ________________

Nombre: ______________________________

La mosca

Responde a cada pregunta.

1. Ésta es una mosca. ¿Cuántas patas tiene una mosca? (Haz un círculo.)

   seis tres ocho

2. ¿Cuántos ojos tiene una mosca? (Haz un círculo.)

   dos tres ocho

3. Haz un círculo alrededor de las antenas de la mosca.

4. Colorea el abdomen de la mosca de negro y el tórax de gris.

5. ¿Vuela la mosca? ______________

Name: ______________________________

Fly

Answer each question.

1. This is a fly. How many legs does a fly have? (Circle one.)

   six three eight

2. How many eyes does a fly have? (Circle one.)

   two three eight

3. Circle the antennae of the fly.

4. Color the abdomen of the fly black and the thorax gray.

5. Does the fly fly? ____________

Nombre: ______________________________

La hormiga

Responde a cada pregunta.

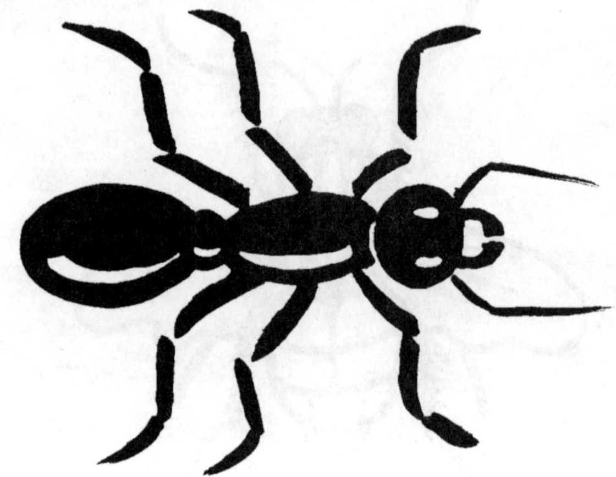

1. Ésta es una hormiga. ¿Cuántas antenas tiene una hormiga? (Haz un círculo.)

   seis dos ocho

2. ¿Cuántos ojos tiene una hormiga? (Haz un círculo.)

   dos tres ocho

3. Haz un círculo alrededor del abdomen de la hormiga.

4. Haz un círculo alrededor de las antenas de la hormiga y coloca una "X" en el tórax.

5. ¿Vuela la hormiga? ______________________________

Name: ______________________________

Ant

Answer each question.

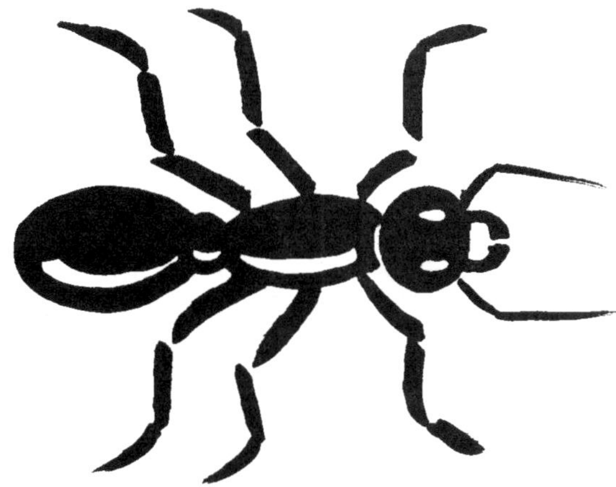

1. This is an ant. How many antennae does an ant have? (Circle one.)

   six two eight

2. How many eyes does an ant have? (Circle one.)

   two three eight

3. Circle the abdomen of the ant.

4. Circle the antennae of the ant and put an "X" on the thorax.

5. Does the ant fly? ___________________________________

Nombre: ______________________________

La mariposa

Responde a cada pregunta.

1. Ésta es una mariposa. ¿Cuántas patas tiene una mariposa? (Haz un círculo.)

   seis tres ocho

2. ¿Cuántos ojos tiene una mariposa? (Haz un círculo.)

   dos tres ocho

3. Haz un círculo alrededor de las antenas de la mariposa.

4. Colorea el abdomen de la mariposa de verde y el tórax de morado.

5. ¿Vuela la mariposa? __________

Name: ______________________________

Butterfly

Answer each question.

1. This is a butterfly. How many legs does a butterfly have? (Circle one.)

   six three eight

2. How many eyes does a butterfly have? (Circle one.)

   two three eight

3. Circle the antennae of the butterfly.

4. Color the abdomen of the butterfly green and the thorax purple.

5. Does the butterfly fly? ___________

Nombre: ______________________________

Colorea las palabras

Lee el cuento. Responde a cada pregunta. Colorea el dibujo.

Las catarinas son insectos pequeños y ovalados. Son rojas con pintas negras o negras con pintas rojas. Como todos los insectos, las catarinas tienen seis patas, dos antenas y ojos compuestos. Las tres partes de su cuerpo son: la cabeza, el tórax y el abdomen.

Las catarinas usan sus alas para escaparse de los pájaros y para atrapar insectos en el jardín.

1. Busca en el cuento las palabras que tienen un acento. Colorea la palabra de rojo.

   ¿Cuántas palabras que tienen acento encuentras?

   ____

2. Usa un creyón de color marrón y colorea todas las palabras que terminan con una "s."

   ¿Cuántas veces encuentras palabras que terminan con la letra "s"? ________________

Name: ______________________________

Color the Words

Read the story below. Answer the questions. Color the picture.

Ladybugs are small, oval-shaped insects. They are red with black spots or black with red spots. Like all insects, they have six legs, two antennae, and compound eyes. The three body parts are the head, the thorax, and the abdomen.

Ladybugs use their wings to help them fly away from birds and to catch garden insects.

1. Look in the story and find all of the words that begin with the letter "h." Color each of these words red.

   How many times did you find and color words with the beginning letter "h"? _______________

2. Use a brown crayon and color all of the words that end with "s."

   How many times did you find words that end with the letter "s"? _______________

Nombre: ______________________________

Colorea las palabras

Lee el cuento. Responde a cada pregunta. Colorea el dibujo.

Las abejas son insectos sociales que viven en colmenas. Como todos los insectos, las abejas tienen seis patas, dos antenas y ojos compuestos. Las tres partes de su cuerpo son: la cabeza, el tórax y el abdomen.

Las abejas tienen alas y pueden volar hasta 15 millas por hora (24 kph). Las abejas chupan néctar de las flores y lo convierten en miel. Las abejas también ayudan a polinizar las flores.

1. Busca en el cuento las palabras que comienzan con la letra "t" y coloréalas de amarillo.

   ¿Cuántas palabras encuentras que comienzan con la letra "t"? ________________

2. Usa un creyón de color verde y busca las palabras que comienzan con la letra "a."

   ¿Cuántas veces encontraste la letra "a"?______________

Name: ___________________________

Color the Words

Read the story below. Answer the questions. Color the picture.

Bees are social insects that live in hives. Like all insects, they have six legs, two antennae, and compound eyes. The three body parts are the head, the thorax, and the abdomen.

Bees have wings and can fly up to 15 miles per hour (24 kph). Bees eat nectar from flowers and turn it into honey. They also help pollinate flowers.

1. Look in the story and find all of the words that begin with the letter "t." Color each of these words yellow.

   How many times did you find and color words with the beginning letter "t"? ____________

2. Use a green crayon and color all of the words that begin with "b."

   How many times did you find words that begin with the letter "b"? ____________

Nombre: ______________________________

Colorea las palabras

Lee el cuento.
Responde a cada pregunta.

Las hormigas son insectos sociales que viven en grupos llamados colonias. Las hormigas pueden ser de diferentes colores—amarillas, marrones, rojas o blancas. Como todos los insectos, las hormigas tienen seis patas, dos antenas y ojos compuestos. Las tres partes de su cuerpo son: la cabeza, el tórax y el abdomen.

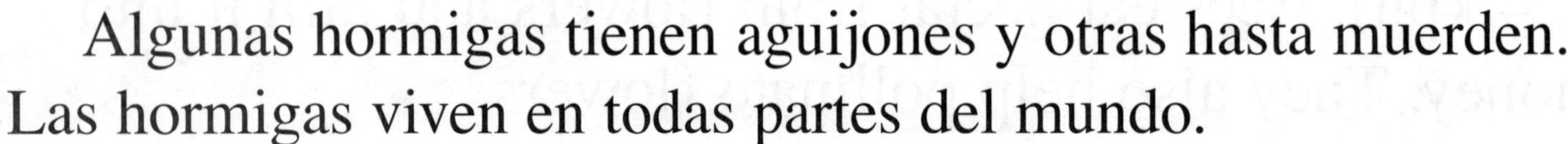

Algunas hormigas tienen aguijones y otras hasta muerden. Las hormigas viven en todas partes del mundo.

1. Busca en el cuento las palabras “el, la, los, las.” Cada vez que encuentres las palabras “el, la, los, las” coloréalas de amarillo. ¿Cuántas palabras “el, la, los, las” descubres en el cuento? _______________

2. Usa un creyón de color verde y colorea todas las palabras “insectos.” ¿Cuántas veces descubres la palabra “insectos”?

   ____

3. Colorea la palabra “dos” de azul. ¿Cuántas veces descubres la palabra “dos”? __________

Name: ______________________________

Color the Words

Read the story below.
Answer the questions.

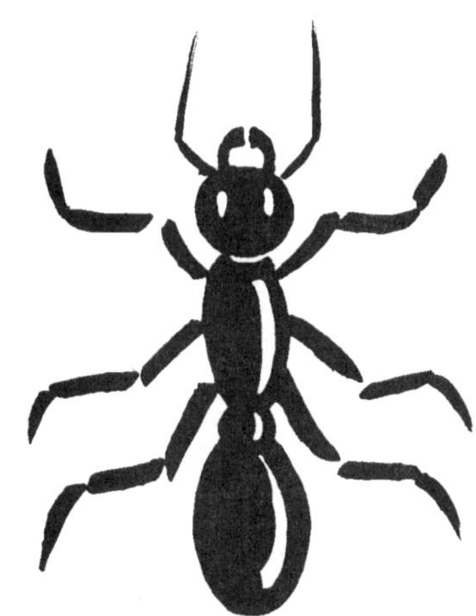

Ants are social insects that live in groups called colonies. They can be many different colors—yellow, brown, red, or black. Like all insects, ants have six legs, two antennae, and compound eyes. The three body parts are the head, the thorax, and the abdomen.

Some ants have stingers, and some even bite. Ants live all over the world.

1. Look in the story and find all of the times the word "the" is used and color it yellow. How many times did you find and color the word "the"? ______________

2. Use a green crayon and color the word "insects" each time it appears. How many times did you find the word "insects"? ______________

3. Color the word "two" blue. How many times did you find the word "two"? ______________

Nombre: ______________________________

Llena los espacios

Escribe la letra que falta en cada palabra.

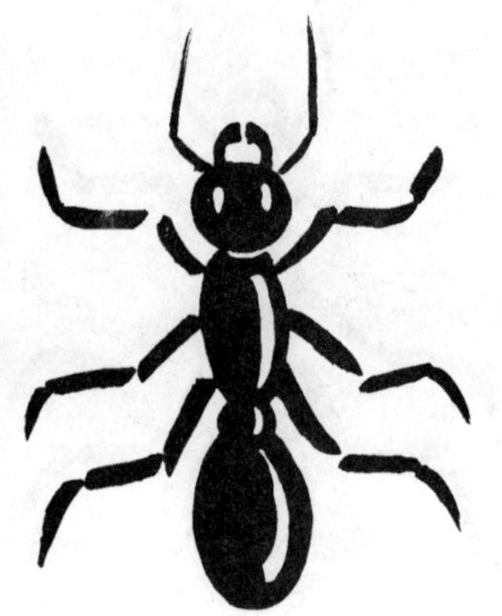

__ormiga

__osca

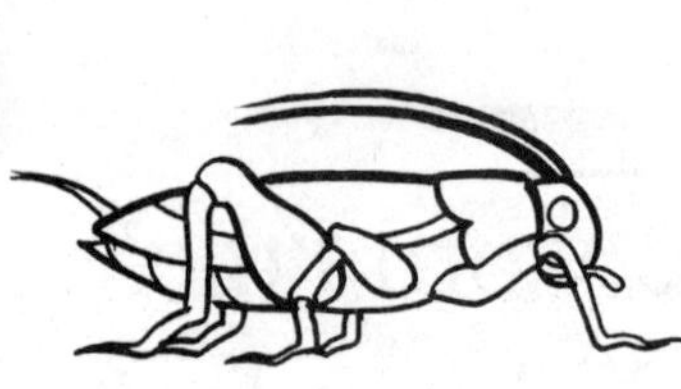

__altamontes

__ariposa

__atarina

__beja

Name: ______________________________

Fill in the Blanks

Fill in the missing letter in each word.

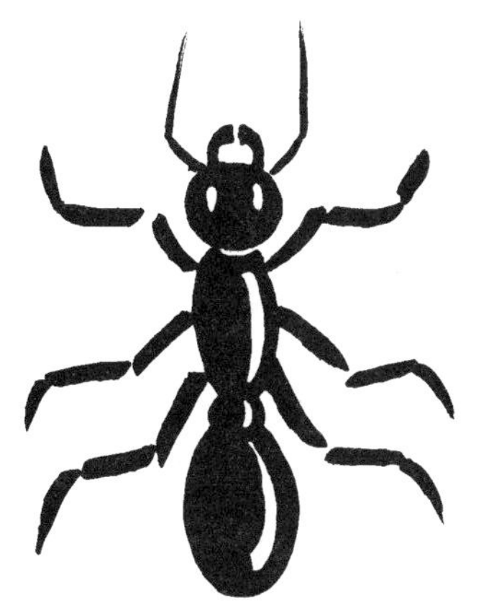

__nt

__ly

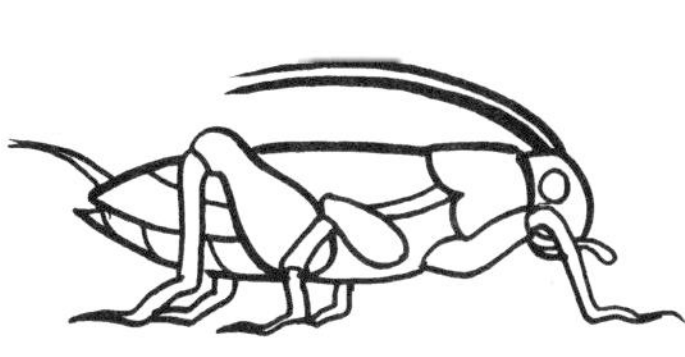

__rasshopper

__utterfly

__adybug

__ee

Nombre: ______________________________

Llena los espacios

Escribe la letra que falta en cada palabra.

sal__amontes

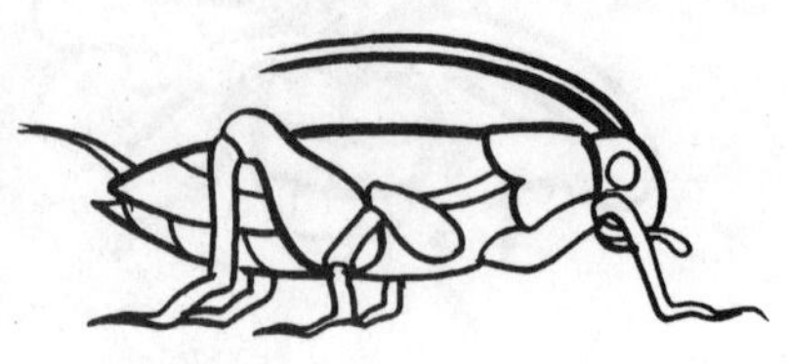

ab__ja

mar__posa

mo__ca

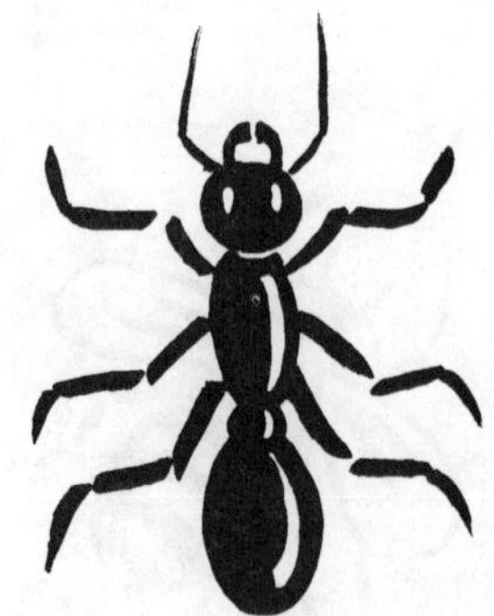

ho__miga

cat__rina

Name: ___________________________

Fill in the Blanks

Fill in the missing letter in each word.

gra__shopper

b__e

but__erfly

f__y

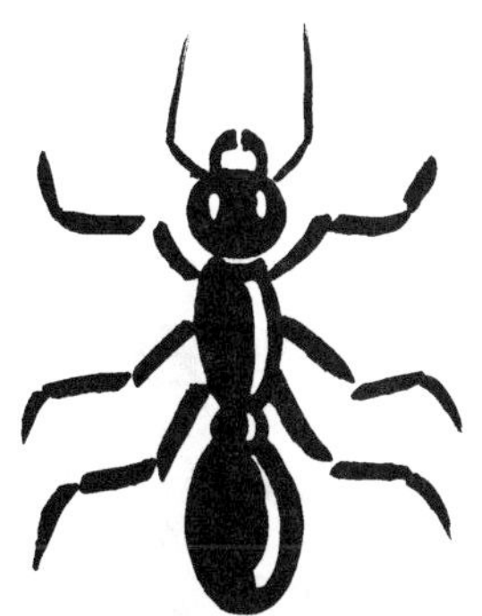

a__t

la__ybug

Nombre: ______________________________

Llena los espacios

Escribe la letra que falta en cada palabra.

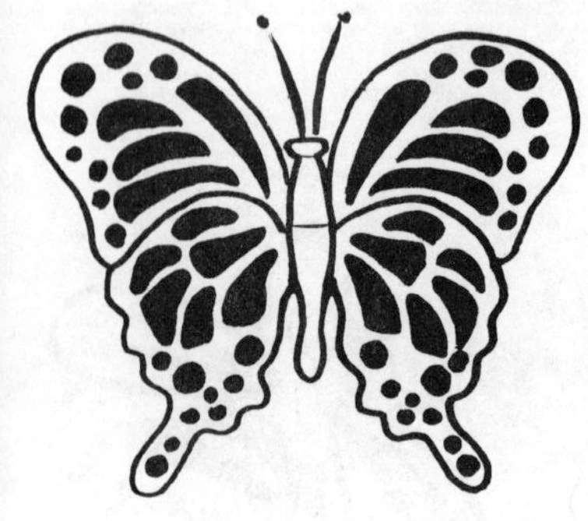

maripos__

mosc__

catarin__

abej__

saltamonte__

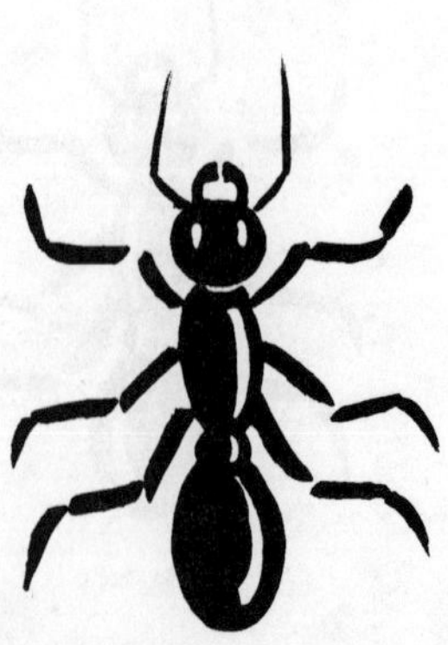

hormig__

Name: ______________________________

Fill in the Blanks

Fill in the missing letter in each word.

butterfl__

fl__

ladybu__

be__

grasshoppe__

an__

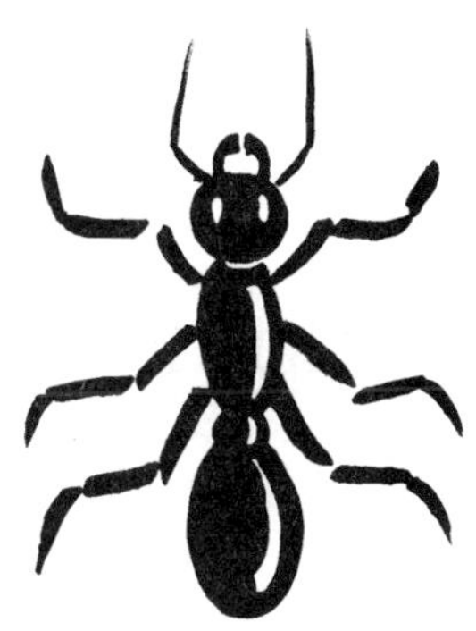

Nombre: ______________________________

Llena los espacios

Llena los espacios con las palabras que siguen para terminar la oración.

1. El tórax, la cabeza y el ________________ son las partes principales de un insecto.
2. Las ____________________ son las partes de un insecto que lo ayudan a oler.
3. Las antenas de un insecto salen de la ________________.
4. Algunos insectos tienen ____________ otros no.
5. Los insectos tienen ______________ patas.
6. Las patas de un insecto salen del __________.
7. Una mariposa es un __________________.
8. Una __________________ no es un insecto.
9. Un insecto tiene dos ______________.
10. Un insecto tiene tres partes principales en su ________________.

Palabras

abdomen	seis	cuerpo	antenas
alas	ojos	tórax	cabeza
	araña	insecto	

Name: ______________________________

Fill in the Blanks

Use the word bank below to complete each sentence.

1. The thorax, the head, and the ________________ are the main parts of an insect.
2. An insect's _______________________ help it smell.
3. The antennae of an insect are attached to its _________________.
4. Some insects have ____________ and others do not.
5. Insects have __________________ legs.
6. The legs of an insect are attached to its __________________.
7. A butterfly is an _____________________.
8. A _______________________ is not an insect.
9. An insect has two _____________________.
10. An insect has three main _________________ parts.

Word Bank

abdomen	six	body	antennae
wings	eyes	thorax	head
	spider	insect	

Answer Key

Pages 54–55
1. 7, 2. Students should color the ladybug red and the fly in the center blue. 3. 9, Equation: 7 + 2 = 9

Page 56
1. seis, 2. cuatro, 3. Students should circle the grasshopper's head. 4. Students should color the grasshopper's abdomen green and its thorax red. 5. sí

Page 57
1. six, 2. four, 3. Students should circle the grasshopper's head. 4. Students should color the grasshopper's abdomen green and its thorax red. 5. yes

Page 58
1. seis, 2. dos, 3. Students should circle the ladybug's head. 4. Students should color the ladybug's abdomen green and its thorax blue. 5. sí

Page 59
1. six, 2. two, 3. Students should circle the ladybug's head. 4. Students should color the ladybug's abdomen green and its thorax blue. 5. yes

Page 60
1. seis, 2. dos, 3. Students should circle the fly's antennae. 4. Students should color the fly's abdomen black and its thorax gray. 5. sí

Page 61
1. six, 2. two, 3. Students should circle the fly's antennae. 4. Students should color the fly's abdomen black and its thorax gray. 5. yes

Page 62
1. dos, 2. dos, 3. Students should circle the ant's abdomen. 4. Students should circle the ant's antennae and put an "X" on its thorax. 5. Las hormigas machos pueden volar.

Page 63
1. two, 2. two, 3. Students should circle the ant's abdomen. 4. Students should circle the ant's antennae and put an "X" on its thorax. 5. Male ants can fly.

Page 64
1. seis, 2. dos, 3. Students should circle the butterfly's antennae. 4. Students should color the butterfly's abdomen green and its thorax purple. 5. sí

Page 65
1. six, 2. two, 3. Students should circle the butterfly's antennae. 4. Students should color the butterfly's abdomen green and its thorax purple. 5. yes

Page 66
1. 3 palabras, 2. 32 veces

Page 67
1. 3 times, 2. 12 times

Page 68
1. 6 palabras, 2. 10 veces

Page 69
1. 12 times, 2. 4 times

Page 70
1. 9 palabras, 2. 2 veces, 3. 1 vez

Page 71
1. 5 times, 2. 2 times, 3. 1 time

Page 72
hormiga, mosca, saltamontes, mariposa, catarina, abeja

Page 73
ant, fly, grasshopper, butterfly, ladybug, bee

Page 74
saltamontes, abeja, mariposa, mosca, hormiga, catarina

Page 75
grasshopper, bee, butterfly, fly, ant, ladybug

Page 76
mariposa, mosca, catarina, abeja, saltamontes, hormiga

Page 77
butterfly, fly, ladybug, bee, grasshopper, ant

Page 78
1. abdomen, 2. antenas, 3. cabeza, 4. alas, 5. seis, 6. tórax, 7. insecto, 8. araña, 9. ojos, 10. cuerpo

Page 79
1. abdomen, 2. antennae, 3. head, 4. wings, 5. six, 6. thorax, 7. insect, 8. spider, 9. eyes, 10. body